THE VILLE OI

Its history & bygones

by

ALFRED T. WALKER

**FOURTH EDITION
REVISED & REPRINTED 1999**

Printed by
Martell Press Limited, Ramsgate, Kent
Fourth Edition 1999

Copyright, 1991, Ann Linington
ISBN 0 9518659 0 0

COVER PICTURE: The earliest known drawing of Birchington Square and Birchington Church drawn by the Rev. James Mickleburgh *who was Curate at Birchington 1830-34 when the Rev. P. Whist was Vicar of Monkton which included Birchington.*

ALFRED T. WALKER

PREFACE

My father the late Alfred Thomas Walker wrote this History as a result of the many requests he received from so many people who expressed a desire to know more about the past of Birchington. He wished to place on permanent record the result of his researches into The History of the Ville of Birchington.

He was Parish Archivist and had access to the many Parish records which have thrown so much light on the past of Birchington.

It gave him great pleasure to transcribe most of the old documents, specially the Church Wardens' Accounts dating from 1531, the Poor Books dating from 1611 and the Parish Registers of Baptisms, Marriages and Burials dating from 1538.

My father was a Sidesman, Server and Church Warden of All Saints' Church, Birchington and associated with Crispe Charity for many years.

He became Head Teacher of Park Lane School, Birchington in 1932 and left in 1938 to become Head Teacher of Salmestone School, Margate where he remained until he retired in 1967, finding more time then to research and write The Ville of Birchington.

This fourth edition is the result of so many people wishing to know more about Birchington and being unable to purchase a copy of The Ville of Birchington, as it was out of print. The index was kindly compiled by Miss J. Burgess who took over the duties of Parish Archivist to All Saints' Church, Birchington from my Father. I am greatly indebted to her for allowing me to use it.

1999   Ann Linington

CONTENTS

PAGE

How Birchington got its name	1
Pre-historic Birchington	3
The Records of Birchington	6
Birchington as a Non-Corporate Limb of the Cinque Port of Dover	15
The Ancient Port of Gore-End and Minnis Bay	21
Quex and its Owners	26
The Kidnapping of Henry Crispe, Esq., of Quekes	34
Birchington part of the Manor of Monkton	39
The Churches and Chapels of Birchington	42
The Quakers in Birchington	51
The Coming of the King to Quex	53
The Cage, the Stocks and the Whipping Post	55
The Maypole	58
The Wax House in Birchington	59
How the Plague hit Birchington	63
How Birchington cared for its Poor	68
The Birchington Workhouse, the Poor's House, the Almshouses	74
Some old Taxes of Birchington	82
Vermin and its destruction in the Vill of Birchington	85
The Agricultural Riots of 1830 — Birchington and Acol Men & a Woman sentenced to be transported	87
The Birchington Schools	92
The Story of the Church Clock	102
Gabriel Charles Dante Rossetti in Birchington	105

Smugglers and Coastguards in Birchington	115
The Bounds of the Parish and the Beating of the Bounds	120
The Old Roads and Trackways of Birchington	123
The Old Birchington Institute — The Village Centre of One Hundred years ago	132
The Story of Birchington's Dog Acre	134
The Story of the Fountain in the Square	136
The Railways of Birchington	140
Some Interesting Houses in Birchington	143
The Bungalows of Birchington	158
The Birchington with Acol Charities	160
Birchington in the Mid 19th Century — Extracts from the Autobiography of Mr. James Pointer	164
The Church of St. Nicholas at Wode — Woodchurch	172
Bibliography	176

THE SQUARE, BIRCHINGTON, 1920.

HOW BIRCHINGTON GOT ITS NAME

The origin and meaning of the name Birchington is referred to by nearly all historians of Kent. In most old documents relating to this place, such as the Churchwardens' Account Books dating from 1531, the Poor Books dating from about 1607 and documents relating to Birchington as a Non-Corporate Limb of the Cinque Port of Dover, Birchington is referred to as The Ville of Birchington.

The word "Ville" or "Vill" or "Vil", is an old Anglo-Saxon French word really meaning a Village or Parish. It was a territorial unit or division under the feudal system consisting of a number of houses or buildings with their adjacent lands. It really corresponds to Parish. In most of the old records, the surrounding villages are referred to as Villes, such as, the Ville of Wood (Acol), the Ville of Sarre, the Ville of Monkton, etc.

The word Birchington is really Saxon in origin. The authority on the Place Names of Kent is J.K. Wallenberg of Uppsala University, Sweden, who published in 1934 his book, "The Place Names of Kent." According to him the earliest known document with the name of our village is the Assize Rolls for Kent of 1240, when the name appears as "de Birchilton".

In the Assize Rolls of 1254 it appears as "de Bruchinton", "de Berchinton" and "Bircheton". In the Patent Rolls of the reign of Henry III, 1264, it appears as "Bercelton".

In the Feet of Fines of Kent of 1274 it is "Byrchelton". A Fine is a record of a Final Agreement or settlement in a common law action relating to land. The Foot is the record's triplicate copy which was filed in the Court of Common Pleas and are now kept in the Public Record Office.

In the Assize Rolls of 1278 it is called "de Berchihton", and in the Feet of Fines of 1292 it appears as "Byrcheton".

From these, Wallenberg suggests that the name is Old English. "Bierce" is Old English for birch (trees) "Hyl" is a slight hill or rising ground. "Tun" is Old English and meant a village which grew up round a farm or manor.

So the name means the village on the rising ground in the birch trees. Birchington is on slightly rising ground and we still have Church Hill.

It must be remembered that in early times Thanet was much more wooded than now. Hasted, the Kent Historian, says that "anciently there was more woodland in Thanet and several villes still preserve the memory of these woods, viz, Woodchurch, Acol or Acholte, a grove of oak trees, Westwood, Northwood and Southwood."

Philpott, who published his "Villara Cantianum" in 1670, considers the name was originally Bircheton, the enclosure where the birch trees grow.

The Oxford Dictionary of English Place Names by E. Kwall says of Birchington, "Bircheton", the Tun among the birches.

The change from Birchilton to Burchenton can be accounted for by the Saxon manner of forming the plural by adding en, as in oxen, brethren, children, housen, and a further change to Birchington would be a case of alteration in the spelling.

The following are some of the many different ways the name is spelt in the old records:—
Birchynton, Byrchynton, Byrchyntone, Bychenton, Bychinton, Birchinyetonne, Birchingetonn, Bircheingetonn, Burchenyetonn, Burcheton, Burchenton, Birchenton and many more.

In the early days there was no standard spelling so whoever kept the records, and it was usually the Minister, spelt the name as he said it and thought it should be spelt.

Acol is also referred to as a Vill. According to Wallenberg, the name appears in the Assize Rolls of 1270 as "de Acholt", also in 1304 Assize Rolls as "de Acholte" and in the Feet of fines of 1343 as Acholte.

So it is Old English made up of:— ac — oak and holt — a wood.

When the church of St. Mildred at Acol was dedicated in 1876 by the Bishop of Dover, in his sermon he referred to the name, "in the oak wood".

Birchington was part of the Hundred of Ringsloe which comprised the Isle of Thanet and is Saxon in origin. The site of the Hundred meeting place is not known but possibly the meeting place was at Mount Pleasant where roads from all parts of the Hundred including Birchington converge.

PRE-HISTORIC BIRCHINGTON

Aerial photography has shown that there are very many Pre-historic sites in Thanet but only a few have been properly scientifically excavated. The Isle of Thanet Archaeological Unit has excavated some sites and published reports. The Unit excavated a Neolithic and Bronze Age site at Lord of the Manor, Haine Road, Ramsgate in 1976-77, but all over Thanet are sites of Pre-historic, Roman and Anglo-Saxon settlements which should be excavated when time and finances allow.

In Birchington a very important Pre-historic settlement was discovered at Minnis Bay in 1938 by a James Beck, a scholar of King's School, Canterbury, who was interested in archaeology. On the foreshore at Minnis, between high and low water marks, some 210 yards from the promenade, his attention was first drawn to a rusty piece of, what he thought at first was, iron sticking out of the sand, which later proved to be a portion of a Bronze Age sword. This led to further discoveries and to a Pre-historic settlement near what would have been the edge of the old coast line and of what later became the port of Gore-end. This settlement dates from at least 1000 years B.C.

James Beck describes his finds in the Kings School Magazine of December 1938, "The Cantuarian". In this he says, "In the Easter holidays of 1938 I came across eight Roman holes from two to five feet deep filled with Roman pottery, and bones of boar, red deer, etc. Whilst unearthing these bones I happened to dig up a bronze knife, only a small piece and green with age. Later I came across a beautiful bronze celt, an instrument rather like an axe used for cutting. There is a socket for a piece of wood to drop into and an eye or handle rather like a cup handle, but very small. This is for a piece of deer thong to be attached and tied firmly to the wood."

Later, James Beck came across many more bronze things, celts, palstaves, dagger points, bracelets, swords, etc. and beside these bronze articles there was much pottery, very rough and uneven in thickness, black or grey.

Later, Mr. F. H. Worsfold, F.S.A., an eminent archaeologist who lived in Birchington, and the British Museum and the Powell Cotton Museum continued the research.

Mr. Worsfold in his report in the Pre-historic Society Journal for 1940 stated that flints ranging from Palaeolithic to Neolithic Periods have been found in the Birchington locality, whilst in the Flats directly facing Minnis Headland, pottery of Roman, Jutish and Saxon character have been found. He says that during the late Bronze Age the present Minnis Bay Flats formed the floor of a seaward extension of the valley flanked on the one hand by the Minnis Bay Headland and on the other by the Rifle Range land, both of which stretched considerably further out in the Thames Estuary than they do now. The site could only be excavated between tides which imposed a severe limitation on the excavations. The silts excavated from the site were examined at the Cambridge Botany School, which supported the idea that here at Minnis Bay was a harvesting working floor with its adjacent pits for the storing of the crops. The pits yielded remains of rushwork or straw arranged thatch wise and embedded in grey silt. Also were found pottery, animal bones, mostly of ox, flint scrappers, sherds and an extensive amount of wattle work, evidently the collapsed walling of dwellings was recovered from many parts of the settlement. The wattle work was composed mainly of interlocking hazel rods. Also other timbers were found, probably the remains of collapsed buildings.

Major P. H. G. Powell Cotton and Mr. G. F. Pinfold of Quex, describe the Pre-historic and Roman site on the foreshore at Minnis Bay in Archaeologiia Cantiana, Vol. L1, (1940) first found by James Beck. Miss Antoinette Powell Cotton also helped in the investigations. Among the items found, as listed in this article are, a Roman millstone, Belgic and Roman pottery, Bronze Age celts and palstaves, bones of deer and ox, heating stones and pot boilers, swords, daggers, spearheads, rings, armulets, bracelets etc.

James Beck suggested that this was the site of a Bronze Age village built round an open space on the bank of a stream that flowed out at Minnis Bay when the land was at a higher level.

The find suggests that the site was occupied from Pre-historic times several thousand years ago, through the Belgic Period, to the Roman times, and to early Saxon times, and even to the early Middle Ages.

Many of the finds are now in the British Museum and some in the Powell Cotton Museum where they are on display in special cases.

Unfortunately James Beck died in 1941.

The late Miss Powell Cotton continued her investigations on the eroded foreshore at Minnis Bay and had found late Bronze Age pottery, remains of leather objects and a red deer antler mount, in pits which had formed part of the habitation complex first investigated by James Beck and Mr. Worsfold. She had also found first century pottery, wooden and bone objects and a small brooch. She had also found pots of different sizes dating from Roman times to the early Middle ages. These are on display in the Powell Cotton Museum.

A few other discoveries of ancient relics have been made in Birchington. In 1853 a discovery of "tin money" was made at Quex. These coins of tin were probably made in the time of the Romans for the use of the Britons. They are in the Powell Cotton Museum.

A hoard of bronze palstaves was found in 1904 in Southend Brickfield, now part of the Park Lane Primary School playing field. These were in an earthen bowl about three feet below the surface.

A Bronze Age palstave was also found at Epple near the Epple Bay Brickfield. Miss Powell Cotton had found Roman and Medieaval wells at Minnis, some probably the base of wells which were in existence before the cliff was eroded.

There are only a few traces of Roman occupation of Birchington, except at Minnis. In 1896, during the erection of Beaconsfield, in what is now Alpha Road, were found three skeletons with a small Roman vase. Roman funeral urns have been found at Quex and Gore-end.

Anglo Saxon remains have been found in the area especially at Sarre. So a settlement has been at Birchington for several hundreds of years, perhaps even thousands.

THE RECORDS OF BIRCHINGTON

THE OLDEST IN THANET AND EAST KENT

Birchington possesses one of the finest and most valuable collections of records and documents, outside Canterbury Cathedral, in East Kent, and if the documents relating to Birchington in the care of the Kent County Archives Office at Maidstone are added, no other similar place in South East England is as well documented. The records are of considerable historical value and extend over 500 years. The records are unique as some date from before the time of the Reformation and so throw some light on the progress of the Reformation in Birchington. They give much information on what Birchington and its people were like through the years.

THE RECEIPTS FOR COMPOSITION MONEY

The oldest documents are the Receipts for Composition Money paid to Dover. From the early 1200's, Birchington with Gore-end was a Non-Corporate Limb of the Cinque Port of Dover and came under the jurisdiction of the Mayor and Jurats of that place. Dover appointed a Deputy — usually the most important person in the place — who was charged with the collection of the Dover sess, or rate, or Composition Money, and to carry out other important official business. The earliest receipt for Composition Money from the Deputy to Dover dates from 1490. It is in Latin for the sum of 16s 8d. This sum was used mainly to help fit out a ship for the King's navy. Attached to these receipts is the seal of Dover — of St. Martin on horseback dividing his cloak and giving one half to a beggar.

The most interesting of these receipts is the Armada Sess of 1588 — a rate levied to help fit our ships to fight against the Spanish Armada of 1588. The sess raised £7 12s 6d from 40 ratepayers, all of whose names are recorded. Tradition has it that the Dover ship helped to capture the great galliasse of the Armada fleet at Calais.

John Underdown of Birchington, the Birchington Deputy paid 16s 8d in 1647. In 1648 during the Commonwealth Period, Birchington had to pay to Dover the sum of £16 13s 9d to help support garrisons at Sandwich, Dover, Walmer, Deal and Sandown. At this time Dover Castle and East Kent were in the hands of the Parliament forces.

THE PARISH REGISTERS

The Parish Registers of Baptisms, Marriages and Burials — 25 volumes — are the oldest in Thanet and date from 1538 — the time of King Henry

VIII to the present day. From the number of entries each year considerable information can be obtained as to the size of the Ville, and considerable help in tracing family trees. Up to 1618 the entries are in Latin, and up to 1837 the time of the passing of the Births and Registration Act and Marriage Act, when registrations became the concern of the civil authorities, the registers have been transcribed and indexed.

The first entry in the Baptism Register of 1538, in Latin is "22° die mensis Novembris baptizata erat Cecilia filia John Cantis." Translated is, 22nd day of the month of November was baptized Cecilia daughter of John Cantis. Cantis is one of the oldest names in Birchington and dates back to about 1300. Members of the family held the important positions of Churchwarden, Overseer and Surveyor over and over again. But like so many babies at this time little Cecilia only lived 4 months for the first entry in the Burial Register is 1538 "Imprimis Cecilia filia Johis Cantis Jun sepulta erat 15 Martj." Translated, First Cecilia daughter of John Cantis Junior was buried 15 March. It must be noted that at this time the year started on 25th March, on the Feast of the Annunciation, so her burial on 15th March was still 1538.

In the Burial Registers are recorded the burials of several of the Crispe family of Quex and of Ministers who served at Birchington Church. In 1678 are recorded Burials in Woollen. The purpose of this Act was to increase the woollen manufacture in England and lessen the import of linen. It was enacted that no corpse should be buried in any material than sheep's wool only and an affidavit was required to be made that the Act had been complied with. In the Registers are a large number of certificates stating that the burial was in woollen. From the Burial Registers can be ascertained when there were epidemics and plagues. Up to the mid 19th century the average number of burials was between 12 and 20, but in 1544 there were 50 burials — a year of plague and in 1637 there were 64 burials — and many of these are marked in the Register as having the plague.

The first entry in the Marriage Register is of the marriage of Robert Chapman and Ursula who were married 13th October 1538 — this is in Latin. At this time it was not the custom to give the bride's surname.

THE CHURCHWARDENS' ACCOUNTS

These accounts date from 1531 and are the oldest in Thanet and are among the oldest in the country, and they continue until the present day. They have been transcribed and indexed, mainly the work of the late Mr. Cyril Coles. They contain an enormous amount of information about the village, and from them it is possible to build up a picture of Birchington in centuries past, the changes in the manners and customs of the village. In early times the Churchwardens were the most important dignitaries in the parish, and had in addition to their church duties, had many civil duties now carried out by the local Council.

The original book commenced in a very humble and small fashion, the entire cost being twopence.

1531 "Item for one quaye of baber to make the boyke of the churche iid." From the regularity of the writing it seems as if the same scribe was employed for years to enter the accounts, and sixpence was paid to him annually. It was probably the Minister who entered the amounts in the accounts. Here is the expenditure of Thomas Pettet and John Wigsell, who were the Churchwardens for 1531.

"Itm for iii pyint of oylle	vid
Itm for one quayr of baber to make the boyke of the churche	iid
Itm to Hary Loyf & Wylliam Lityllwood for wachying of the sepulkyre	iiiid
Itm for berying of the stro to the churche	iid
Itm to the p(ro)cession of Wodchurche in brayd & drynke	vid
Itm for strekyng of the cross lyghte xxv li and a halfe of olde waxe meyt & drynke & streking	xvd
Reme(m)ber iii li of newe waxe of Thomas Pettet	
Itm for strekyng of the trinite lyghte"	

Watching the Sepulchre took place at Easter time. The Sepulchre was a small rectangular hollow on the north side of the east wall of the Chancel of the Church and made to resemble a tomb. On the evening of Good Friday the Crucifix and Host were placed in the sepulchre with much ceremony and watchers stood by until the dawn of Easter Day. Then the Crucifix and Host were removed to the altar with much praise. For watching the sepulchre Harry Love and William Littlewood received one groat.

At this time the floor of the church was earth and so as to give it some semblance of warmth it was covered with straw which was changed at the great festivals.

The procession of Woodchurch refers to the beating of the bounds, when the parish officers with others went to the extent of the parish to Acol and were regaled with refreshments.

In 1533 is found this interesting entry,

"Itm ryngyng at the tempes(t) to Thomas
Norman   iid"

THE CHURCHWARDENS' ACCOUNT BOOK
The first page for 1531

Thomas Norman was the Minister at Birchington at the time. It was thought that by ringing the bells at the time of storms was a protection.

The receipts of the Churchwardens, Thomas Pettet and Moreys Cacherell for 1532 show the source of the Church income. It came from income from land, shops and houses, from renting out sheep and cows, and from "obits". Obits were receipts and payments made on the anniversary of the death of a person of note.

Here is a selection of the receipts of Thomas Pettet and Moreys Cacherell, Churchwardens for 1532.

"Itm of Rychard Ca(n)tes for ferm of scheppe	iiiis
Itm of Harre Baker for ferm of scheppe	iiiis
Itm of Laurence Martyn for ferm of one kowe	iis
Itm of John Jonson for ferm of one kowe	iis
Itm of Thomas Lynkolle for one kowe	iis
Itm of the land of Johne Cacherell	iis
Itm of John Bouchrye for hys schoppe	iis
Itm of Wylliam Steyll for hys schoppe	iis
Itm of Fr Cuthbert for hys house	viiis
Itm of Rychard Ca(n)tes for the groynd besyde the p(ar)sonage	iid
Itm of Johne Ca(n)tes the elder for the obyit of Mast Viacre	xxd "

Sheep and cows were farmed out by the Churchwardens, pledges being expected for their safe custody. In 1532 it appears the Church owned 5 cows and 24 sheep and about 13 acres of land, also one house and two shops. The house was occupied by the Minister. One shop was probably a butcher's shop, and still is a butcher's shop to-day. In 1535 the Churchwardens sold a cow to Johne Norwod for xiiiis xid. Some 40 years later, when a cow was purchased to renew the Church stock, it cost 40 shillings. Prices had advanced considerably. From 1576 a Sess or rate was levied on the parish for the repair of the Church, up to 1700 on acreage from ½d to 3d per acre, and after that date from 1d to 1s in the pound.

10

From these accounts information can be gleaned on the following,

The Church Fabric — its repair, the re-shingling of the steeple, re-glazing of the windows and white-washing of the interior.

The weather vane — and the re-gilding.

The interior of the Church — before and after the Reformation - candles, lights, images, rood, straw, wax and the wax house, altars and their pulling down, burials in the Church, and lighting of the Church.

The Organ and the Parish Chest, also the Kings Arms, the Sentences, the seats and pews.

The bells — the number, re-casting, ringing on special events.

The Churchyard and Church property.

The Dog whipper, the Stocks and the Maypole.

Wages and prices.

The destruction of Vermin.

Acol and Woodchurch, and beating the bounds.

Poll Tax, Window Tax, Chimney Tax.

Sesses — with lists of inhabitants and amounts paid etc. etc.

Altogether there are 5 volumes of Accounts, a veritable gold mine of information on the village through the ages.

THE VOW AND COVENANT AND THE SOLEMN LEAGUE AND COVENANT

Birchington possesses two very rare documents, The Vow and Covenant and the Solemn League and Covenant of 1643, the time of the Civil War. They are rare because in 1661 at the Restoration of Charles II all copies were ordered to be burnt but Birchington preserved its copies. There are only five copies left in Kent. The Vow and Covenant, in the handwriting

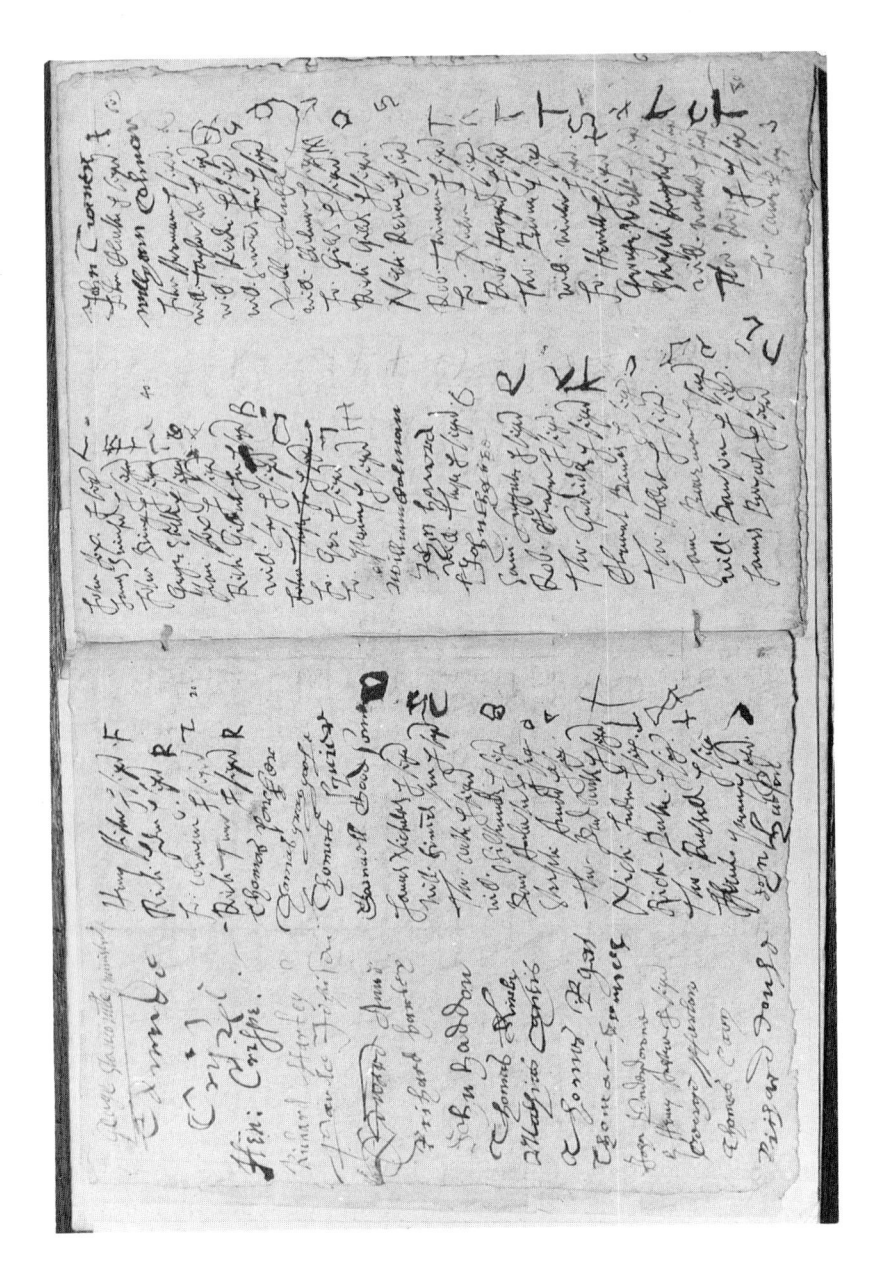

THE VOW AND COVENANT, 1643
Showing the signatures and marks of the men of Birchington.

of Mr. Stancombe, the Minister at the time, was read in the Church on two Sundays by him, after which it was signed by all the men of the village present over 18 years of age. One hundred and seventy one men signed and of these 129 made marks as they were unable to write their names. All who signed promised to assist the forces raised by Parliament against the forces raised by King Charles I.

The Solemn League and Covenant was read and signed the following March, 1643/4. On this occasion 168 men raised their right hands in assent when Mr. Stancombe read it from the pulpit and then signed or made their marks.

(The signatures to the Vow and Covenant read in Birchington Parish Church on 10th and 17th July 1643)

George Stancombe Minister	Henry Fisher I signed F
	Rich. Jurden I signed R
Edward Crispe	Jo. Coleman I signed Z
Hen. Crispe	Rich Turner I signed R
Richard Hartey	Thomas Parker
Paule Johnson	Thomas Graygoose
Edward Anne	Thomas Squier
Richard Hartey	Samuell Goodsonn
John Haddon	James Nicholas I signed
Thomas Kirby	Will. Simes Sen I signed
Mathias Cantis	Tho. Cooke I signed
Thomas Rogers	Will. Silkewood I signed
Thomas ?	David Furburton I signed
John Underdowne	Stephen Arnold I signed
Henry Austen I signed	Tho. Bedbrooke I signed
George Marlow Thomas Carey	Nich Jurden I signed
Thomas Carey	Rich Duke I signed
Richard Douse	Tho. Russell I signed
	Francis Penney I signed
	John Hutson

THE POOR BOOKS

Birchington also possesses a number of Poor Books, for the Ville of Wood (Acol) as well as for Birchington. These date from 1611 and are the accounts of the Churchwardens and the Overseers of the Poor recording their receipts and disbursements in the relieving of the poor of the two parishes. These books also throw much light on the history of Birchington during nearly 300 years from 1611. These have been transcribed. By the Poor Law of Elizabeth I, 1601, the parish became responsible for the appointment of Overseers of the Poor, and for an imposition of a rate or sess to assist the Churchwardens in maintaining the widows, orphans, the impotent, the unemployed, and the sick. From them we can gather information about the prices of foodstuffs, of articles of clothing, of coal, times of famine, apprenticing orphans etc.

In the archives are a number of documents relating to Birchington as a Non-Corporate Limb of the Cinque Port of Dover, including Settlement Certificates, Apprenticeship Indentures from 1607, documents relating to Birchington Workhouse, the Waywardens Book, documents relating to the Church fabric, the Church Bells, the Charities, the Church Lands, the Tithe Map and the accompanying schedule, and the Vestry Books. The Tithe Map was drawn up in 1840 as a consequence of the Tithe Act of 1836 which commuted tithe to a corn rent based on the price of wheat, barley and oats over a seven year period. The map shows all fields and houses in the parish and the schedule sets out names of owners, occupiers, the name of the lands, state of cultivation and the amount of rent charge.

The Vestry was in early days the forerunner of the Council of to-day and was concerned with all the principal affairs of the parish. It was so called from the place in which it normally met, the small room set apart in the Church, but in Birchington the Vestry usually met and then adjourned to the local inn, now the Powell Arms.

BIRCHINGTON AS A NON-CORPORATE LIMB OF THE CINQUE PORT OF DOVER

THE WORK OF THE DEPUTY

Birchington for many centuries was a Non-Corporate Limb of the Cinque Port of Dover. Dover was the head port which had a number of "limbs" or members loosely associated with it, some being merely villages and others towns which had secured a royal grant of incorporation — Faversham and Folkestone were Corporate members of Dover whereas Margate, St. Johns, Goresend and Birchington and others were Non-Corporate members.

Being a Non-Corporate limb, Birchington came under the jurisdiction of the Mayor and Juratts of Dover and not under the county. The area under the Mayor and Juratts was known as the "Liberties".

Dover appointed a Deputy in Birchington, a position something like that of a Deputy Mayor to act on behalf of Dover. He was usually one of the leading men of the parish and at first appointed annually. The office of Deputy in Birchington can be traced back for many centuries. It was his duty to collect the levy to be paid to Dover, and to send it to Dover, watch the "passage" of Birchington and not allow anyone to land without taking the oath of loyalty, look after vagrants, and see that all legal documents are sent to Dover for sealing and signing. Documents for Apprentices, Bastardy Orders, Poor Laws Orders etc. all had to be signed and sealed by the Mayor of Dover. In the Birchington records are many documents signed and sealed by the Mayor and Juratts of Dover, the oldest being of the time of Henry VII, 1490, when Richard Fyneaux was the Mayor of Dover, and then there is a receipt dated 1499 when a John Byngham was the Mayor and Johanne Philip was the Deputy in Birchington. Both have part of the seal of Dover attached — that of St. Martin on horseback dividing his cloak and giving one half to the beggar.

It is probable that Birchington with Goresend has been a Limb of Dover since the time of Edward I, that is 1272, and taxed by Dover, usually 16s 8d a year to help fit out ships and men. The Cinque Ports at this time supplied and fitted out the ships for the King's Navy.

It is not clear whether Birchington included Gore-end or if Gore-end included Birchington as a Non-corporate limb. From a document in the Public Record Office it is known that in 1523 Birchington sent four jurors to Dover and that Gore-end and Birchington together sent the same number.

The Birchington jurors were,
>	Thomas Petyst
>	John Wygsall
>	John Sage
>	Richard Cantes

The Goresend and Byrchynton jurors were,
>	Thomas Holden
>	Ricus Cantes
>	Johes Cantes
>	Henry Thorne

Thomas Petyst and John Wygsall were Churchwardens in 1531. It was they who with others made a "rekyng of the churche lands of Birchyntone the XVII yere of Kyng Herry the VIII", that is in 1527. From this list of Church lands it appears that Thomas Pettet, John Wygsall and John Cantes had land in Birchington and that Thomas Holden had land adjoining the "Butts". The Cantes family was an important family in Birchington and members held important offices in the village at different times. John Cantes was Churchwarden in 1537.

Another duty of the Deputy was the taking of prisoners from Birchington to Dover to stand trial and in the accounts are entries for expenses for the journey.

1630 It for my iorney to Dover about ye poore	00 05 00
1631 It to James Sen for 2 ioynies to Dover	00 10 00
1636 It to Jo Crumpe for going to Dover for a warrant for Roger	00 03 00
It to Mr. Stancombe for going to Dover with a petition to Mr. Crispe and Mr. Mayer covering Roser	00 08 06
1652 for horse hire to Dover and their charges for three journeys	00 18 00

In 1526 the Deputy of Birchington and Gore-end paid 16s 8d to Dover towards the cost of Dover's suit for the discharge of a subsidy. On this occasion the Deputy of Mergate and St. Johns paid 26s 8d.

Towards the end of the 16th century, Birchington was almost an agricultural village and Gore-end was little used as a landing place. In the time of Elizabeth I, Special Commissioners made a return of the number of boats, population, houses and officials in the members limbs of the Cinque Ports. Birchington was stated to have 42 inhabited houses and "it had neither shippe nor boate".

In 1584 a Vincent Underdown, deputy, certified that there were but three fishermen at Birchington all of whom were in the habit of sailing from Margate. They were Henry Brabsonne, Ralphe Linche and Stephen Knight.

One of the most valuable documents in the Birchington records is the Armada Sess of 1588. This sess was to raise money to help towards the fitting out of the Dover ships to fight against the Spanish Armada. The amount to be raised was £5 16s 8d but the sess fixed to raise the sum of £6 7s 9d. Forty names of Birchington people are on the list and the amounts paid vary from 3d to 20s.

> The heading of the sess is as follows,
> "A sesse made the XXVIIIth day of April 1588 by the consent of the pissioners of Birchingtone for and concerning the XXIII li VIs VIIId to be paid to the Maior and Jurattes of Dover towards the setting out of their shippes for VIII weekes service as folowethe whereof our pte is V li XVIs VIIId."

Then follows the list of the Birchington people and the amounts paid by each.

In 1610 Mr. Henry Prowe was the Deputy for Birchington and in the records is his receipt for the 16s 8d paid to "ye Maior Juratts and commonalty of the towne and port of Dover."

The office of Deputy was no sinecure as in 1620 the Deputy received the wrath and displeasure of the Lord Warden. One of the Deputy's duties was to assist in the watching of the "passage of Birchington", and not to allow any person to land without taking the oath of allegiance to the King — on this occasions James I. In 1620 it was reported to the Lieutenant of Dover Castle that a passenger had landed at Birchington without having taken the oath. The Lieutenant of Dover Castle sent for the Deputy on the 12th December 1620 and then committed him to prison. Fourteen days later after having spent Christmas in prison he was released on representations because he had erred in ignorance. In those days great precautions and vigilance were required because of the unsettled state of the relations with neighbouring nations.

In Archaeologia Cantiana Volume XII is given the Muster Roll for 1614 showing how the inhabitants of Birchington were called on to furnish men and arms in times of emergency.

Here is the Muster Roll October 12th and 13th, 1614 from the Domestic State Papers James I Vol. 78, No. 32.

	Birchington Corslets	Muskets	Light horses
Sir Henry Crisp Knight	4	4	2
Rich Harters gent	2	2	1
Edwd Knight	3	3	1
Wm Daward	1	1	—
Robert Seath	1	2	—
Vincent Underdown	1	1	Dry Pike 1
Willyam Foord	1	2	—
Robert Cawvill	1	1	—
Henry Culmer	1	—	—

A corslet was a cuirass, formerly the usual body covering of pikemen, chiefly of leather and pistol proof.

In the Domestic State Papers of Charles I, Vol. 108, No. 59, is a list of soldiers and the names of such persons on whom they were billetted in Birchington in 1627 when England was at war against France under Richelieu.

"A tru List of the names of all such soldiers as were lately billitted in Birchington in the Isle of Thanett & also the names of such persons upon whom they were billitted & the tyme of theire Continuance there, viz, from Jan 22 1627 untill Mar 3 An. eodem 6 weekes full.

The names of the Billitters	The names of ye Soldiers billitted
Sir Hen Crispe Knight	Lieutenant Chauntrell & John Little
Henry Couluer	William Benson
Nicholas Sayer	
John Seely	Thomas Mansfield
Henry Hayward	
(These 4 remayned there but one weeke)	
Richard Coleman	Sergeant Peele
Vincent Underdowne	Robert Moore
Thomas Kerby	John Frost
Mathias Cantis	Francis Patricke
Thomas Culmer	Gregory Burgesse
Daniell Friend	Andrew Lamar
Robert Cavell	Nicholas Morris
Arnold Peper	
Paul Elnor	Ralphe Wilde
John Cocke	

Widdow Ambrose	
Widdow Appleton	Richard Stone
Solomon Finus	
Jeffery Reade	Henry Purchas
Edward Coleman	
William Coleman	Walter Griffin
William Jordan	William Morgan
John Crumpe	
Richard Gilbert	

(All these 12 for 6 weekes)

The whole number of Soldiers billetted, there are 15 Soldiers & one Lieutenant of which 12 Soldiers were billitted there 6 weekes and the Lieutenant & 3 soldiers but one weeke.

The 12 Soldiers billetts for 6 weekes at iiis Vid a piece per weeke is Xii li Vlls. The 3 Soldiers billett for one weeke at iiis Vld peace per weeke is xs Vid."

In the Birchington records are a Warrant and a receipt for money for General Livesey, the commander of the Parliamentary forces in Kent during the Civil War. The money was to provide for the soldiers in several garrisons in East Kent. Birchington had to pay £16 13s 9d which George Marlow, the Deputy paid three days after the issue of the Warrant.

The last of the Dover receipts in the records is dated August 1660 when the Deputy Henry Austen paid 50s. This receipt has the Dover seal on it.

Towards the end of the 16th century the Mayor and Justices of the Peace came from Dover usually to Margate, for the Sessions annually when the Deputy was appointed. On these occasions four of the inhabitants of Birchington attended as jurymen.

An interesting case is dated 1680 when John Austen, the Deputy had a case of brawling in Birchington the delinquent being the son of the Churchwarden, John Creak. It was that John Creak, the Churchwarden for Acol who contributed towards the cost of the silver "Birchington Chalice". He did this after several visits to the alehouse and what he spent there on refreshments is duly entered in his account.

Brawling at Birchington
Dover Sessions — Depositions
XXiiii of October 1679. Before Nicholas
Cullen Esq., Maior and Mr. West.

John Ayling, Clerke, Viccar of Birchington on the Isle of Thannett in the Countie of Kent maketh oath.

That John Creake of Birchington afore-said youn

being lately enjoyned penaunce for incontinence came into the parish Church on Sunday last being the 19th of this instant October and did afterwards affront and interrupt me the said Jo. Ayling as I was dictating the words of pennaunce unto him and more particularly when I came to those words "and wee therfore heartily sorry" he p'sently replyed "and are therefore never a whitt sorry" upon which saying of his I left him and would proceed no further in this order.

And afterwards when I came out of the Church into the Churchyard he called me "Lowsy rogue and dog" and sayd he could afford to run his stick down my throat.

Afterwards as I was riding on horseback to the house of Thomas Crispe, Esq. where I dined that day he took up a great stone and threw it at me and hitt me on the hip uttering these words "That if he mett me in another place he would claw my bone for mee", or words to that effect.

Jo. Ayling
Vic of Birchington."

There is a note in the margin that Jo. Creake was discharged from a "recognizaunnce entied upon the affidavit, Mr. Ayling not appearing to prosecute."

In later years Deputies held the office for life if they so desired.

During the 18th and 19th centuries the following have held the office of Deputy,

Mr. John Neame, who occupied part of the Quex lands.
Mr. Francis Neame who resided in a portion of the Old Quex mansion.
Mr. John Friend who lived at Birchington Place (Hall).
Mr. George Taddy Friend.
Mr. William Tomlin.
Mr. John Scoats of Brooks End.
Mr. George Friend.
Mr. Edward Neame who died 1869.
Mr. Thomas Gray of Birchington Place (Hall).

THE ANCIENT PORT OF GORE-END AND MINNIS BAY

The little port of Gore-end, Birchington has vanished, but there was a time in far off days when Gore-end, now known as Minnis Bay, had a haven for shipping. John Leland, the English Antiquary of Henry VIII's time, 1542, has this to say about that part of Birchington now known as Minnis Bay, "Reculver is now scarce half a mile from the shore but is to be supposed that in times past the se cam hard to Gore-end, a two mile from Northmouth, and at Gore-ende is a little straite called Broode Staires to go down the clive (cliff)." He further mentions that vessels lie off Gore-end and find further anchorage in the Roads towards the foreland. From his description of Gore-end there appears to be little, if any, resemblance between that section of the coast as we know it today and the place which John Leland surveyed.

"The little Strait called Broode Staires to go down the clive" has entirely disappeared in the erosion which the sea has made since his day. Erosion has been calculated at approximately two feet a year until the recent building of the coastal defence works from Grenham Bay to Minnis. Since Leland's day in 1542 it has been calculated that over 800 feet of land have gone. If this calculation is carried back to the great storm of 1348 over 1200 feet of land have been eroded. It may have been this great storm and one a little later that completed the destruction of Gore-end as a useful port.

The erosion at Reculver has been almost three times as great as at Gore-end owing to the nature of the subsoil there, (the Thanet Sands) and probably the material so displaced had no doubt to a large extent contributed progressively to the silting up of the Wantsum, the once important seaway from Sandwich, past Sarre and Reculver to the Thames estuary.

The port of Gore-end ran from the chalk headland to the east of Minnis to the lower land where the Rifle Range once existed and now where there are mounds to the west of the Cafe. It ran in a north westerly direction towards the Gore Channel and was shaped somewhat like a wedge. The eastern coastline of the port can be traced running from the Minnis Road along the line where the chalk and the sand meet out towards the remains of the wreck of the "Valkyr". The haven extended inland between the Minnis Road on the east and King Avenue on the west as far as the old farm houses at Lower Gore-end, now known as Old Bay Cottage. Before the earth embankment was constructed along the Parade to where is now Hengist Avenue followed later by the stone embankment constructed in 1879/80, this area was known locally as the "Lagoon".

The Tithe Map of Birchington of 1840 shows this area as a morass of reedy pools which were flooded at high Spring tides. The large scale Ordnance Map of 1872 shows this area as an inlet. This was the stub end of the old haven which stretched much further seawards so forming quite a respectable haven for the small ships of those far off days, with sheltering high ground on either side, specially on the east by the chalk cliffs now eroded.

It was probably the gales which periodically raged with tremendous violence along this stretch of sea coast which created great havoc at Gore-end and Brooks-end, and completed the destruction of Gore-end as a useful port, all trace of which has now disappeared. It had been in existence since Pre-historic times, through the Roman period, the times of the Saxons, and the Normans to the Middle Ages. There was also an inlet up to Brooksend and there probably, a landing place.

The name Gore-end is interesting. From the Oxford Dictionary a "gore" is a wedge shaped piece of cloth adjusting the width of a garment. It is also a triangular piece of land. The word is Old English from "gara" meaning a triangular piece of land. Perhaps it is derived directly from the Saxon word "gara" meaning a projecting point of land which in turn comes from "gar" meaning a spear. As a place name it appears frequently in Kent. Although the present appearance of Minnis Bay or Gore-end seems so unlike a triangular piece of land yet in earlier times that interpretation would have been quite appropriate. The Gore-end or Minnies headland stretched so much further seaward than at present that the "end of a projecting point of land" could well have described the area.

Some idea of the importance of Gore-end can be gauged from the knowledge that it was assessed as a Non-Corporate Limb of the Cinque Port of Dover. It was a Non-Corporate Limb since early times — the time of Edward I (1272-1307). In the Dover Chamberlain's Accounts for 1365-67 appears the following,

> "XIs received from the men of Goreshende in full receipt until the feast of Easter."

This shows that Gore-end was a limb of Dover. In early documents relating to Dover, Gore-end is sometimes included with Birchington and sometimes Birchington with Gore-end. In the time of Henry VIII in 1521 representatives from Birchington and Gore-end attended the General Brotheryeld of the Cinque Ports held at Romney. When Bon-jour Crispe was kidnapped from Quex in 1657 and held to ransom he was taken by ship from Gore-end.

There is a tradition that at Gore-end there was once a church which was destroyed by the "fall of the cliffs, it standing near the sea." This tradition was first put forward by John Harris in his "History of Kent" of 1719. The church was supposed to have stood very near the sea but there is no documentary evidence of such a church at Gore-end. The church referred to is probably that of All Saints at Shuarts excavated in 1978-79 by the Thanet Archaelogical Unit. There was a Pre-historic village at Gore-end situated on that part of the eroded chalk, discovered in 1938.

So the port of Gore-end died and from the late Middle Ages the only houses there were the farm houses of Lower Gore-end. So it remained until the middle of the 1800's — an empty space mainly given over to farming. In about 1818 the first Coast Guard Station was established at St. Nicholas near Plum Pudding Island and was part of the Kent Coast Blockade. The buildings were on the cliff edge, and the children of the Coast Guards living there after 1848 attended the National School in Park Lane, Birchington. In winter when the "way was dangerous" they did not attend school as recorded in the School Log Books. These houses were demolished in about 1860, so Minnis Bay was rather a desolate and lonely appendage of Birchington. In about 1870's the Minnis Bay Coast Guard Cottages with the Captain's house were built which still stand to the east of the Minnis Road not far from the "dip" once part of the Gore-end inlet. They were occupied by Coast Guards until the beginnning of this century — now they are private residences. After the coming of the railway, Minnis Bay like Birchington, began to develop. The man who did much to do this was Mr. A. R. Rayden, a London Stock Broker, assisted by Mr. C. R. Haig. He founded the Birchington Bay Estate Company and he was the leading figure in the spectacular effort to raise money for the Birchington Institute in the Square, by planning the Exhibition held at Minnis in the special Exhibition Building he had built in the "dip". Special trains were run for this exhibition and it was well advertised.

Before the turn of the century two blocks of colonial type houses were built on the Parade. The first shop in Minnis Bay was the present Post Office and General Stores built in 1903. In 1930 two terraces of shops were built and to-day these nine shops and an Off Licence are the only shops in Minnis Bay. The Bay Hotel was built in about 1905 and later, Uncle Tom's Cabin, but these were demolished in the 1960's when the blocks of flats were constructed on the site. Other houses and bungalows were built up to the outbreak of the Second World War when Minnis again became a dead place with defences erected. Some of the early houses were built with bricks from the Brick yard at the end of Ingoldsby Road.

The first time the word "Minnis" appears in any documents is in 1531, the time of Henry VIII, when it appears in the Churchwardens' Account

Book where there is the complete survey of the Church Lands made by the Churchwardens, John Crispe of Quex, Robert Phylipp, Thomas Pettet and Rycharde Cantes. The Churchwardens supplied a full and complete description of the lands owned by the Birchington Church made from a survey of 1527. One piece is described as,

> "The XV pece one akyre of Romescot land at Seegate, Robert Wigsoll east, the Menesse otherwysse called a Comen, south, Robert Phylype north and west."

The word comes from Old English meaning "land held in common". Hasted in his History of Kent suggests that the name may be derived from the Latin word, "mina" signifying both among the Romans and others a certain quantity of land. It has been put forward that it may derive from the French word "demesne" which became spoken of as "maynes" and the transition from this to "minnis" is easy. There is no doubt that minnis was formerly apparently common land.

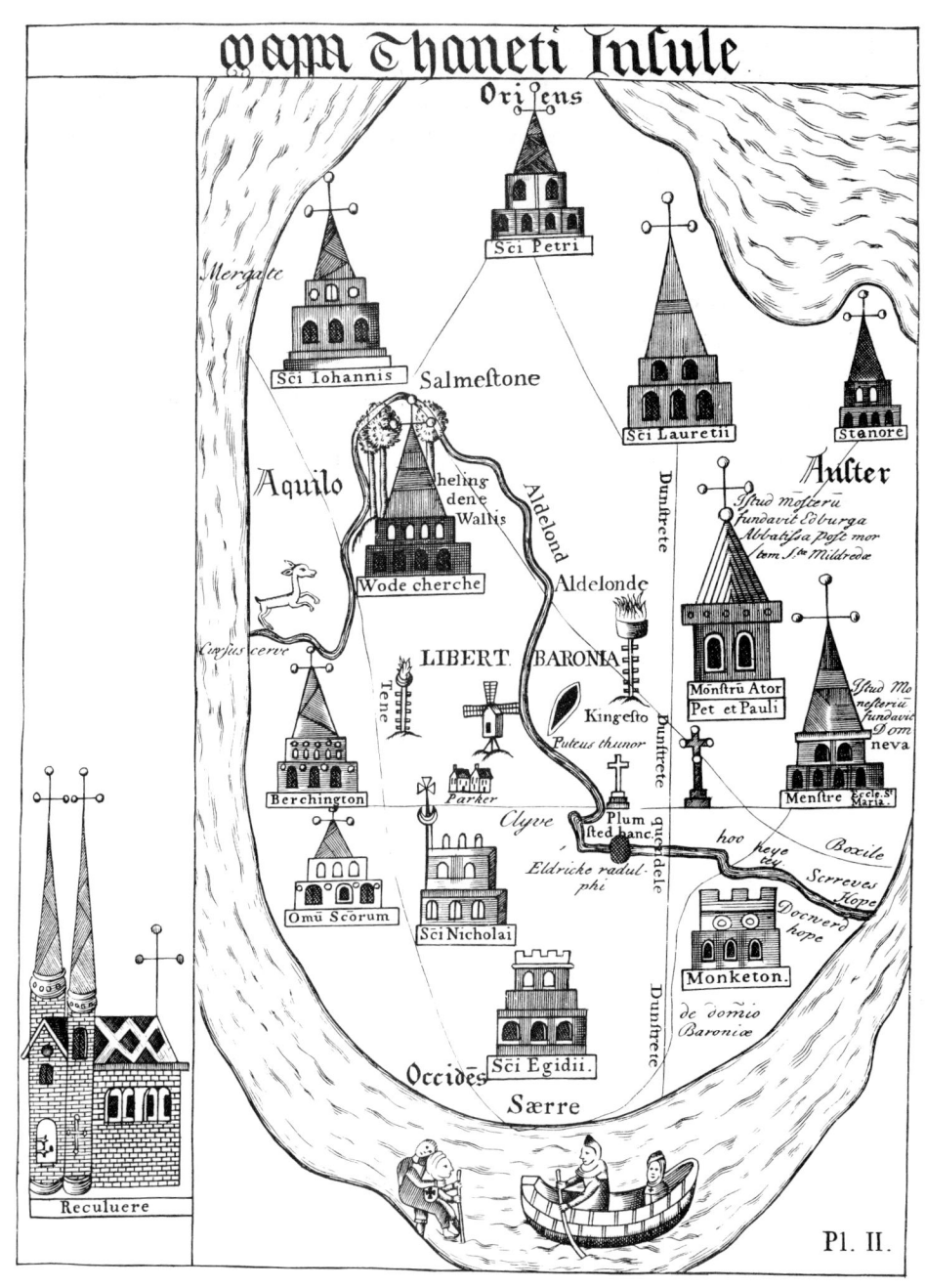

THOMAS OF ELMHAM'S MAP OF THE ISLE OF THANET, cica 1412
Showing Birchington, Woodchurch, All Saints and Parker.

QUEX AND ITS OWNERS

Quekes, Quek or Quex, was the seat of an ancient family which bore that name, but the earliest known owners of Quex were the Parkers. Their residence, called "Parkers" is shown on Thomas of Elmham's map of the Isle of Thanet, which was made about the year 1400. Thomas of Elmham was a monk of St. Augustine's Abbey, Canterbury and the original of the map is at Trinity Hall, Cambridge. This house is no longer in existence but its position is thought to have been very near the present mansion.

In 1411, John Parkere bequesthed £6 to the fabric of the Church of Birchington and in 1418, Cecilia Parkere willed 6s 8d to the Church. She also left legacies to the Lights of St. Mary, now the Quex Chapel, to St. Margaret, now the St. Margaret's Chapel and also to the Lights of the Blessed Mary in the Church at Wode (Woodchurch).

The Parkers were succeeded by the Queks who first appear as occupiers or owners of land in the Isle of Thanet in 1334. There is no record of the transfer of the property to John Quex and it may be that he married the heiress of the Parkers and so obtained possession. It is this John Quex who built the old Manor House of Quex, which, with various alterations and additions made during the course of the centuries, lasted until it was pulled down by John Powell Powell in 1806. In his will this John Quex bequeathed the sum of 10 marcs (£6 13s 4d) for making a window and the glass thereto for the Chancel of St. Mary, now the Quex Chapel in Birchington Church. He died in 1449 and was buried in Quex Chapel where his excellent brass can now be seen showing him in the civil dress of the period with his son as a pigmy by his side.

The ownership of Quex remained with the Quex family for three generations, until the heiress, Agnes Quex, married John Crispe, the second son of Henry Crispe, of Stanlake, Oxfordshire, early in the 16th century, thereupon the Crispes succeeded to the Queks as owners of the largest estate in Thanet.

The Crispe family owned the estate until the year 1707 and produced many interesting, influencial and colourful characters in the history of Birchington, Thanet and Kent. Many of them are buried in the Quex Chapel of Birchington Church where can be seen their brasses, monuments and memorial tablets. Some became Sheriffs of Kent, a most important position in those days.

The most famous of the Crispe family was Sir Henry Crispe, grandson of the first John Crispe and who was known as the King of the Island or Regulus Insulae. He was Churchwarden of Birchington in 1539, when Birchington purchased its first Bible for 20s. He was Sheriff of Kent and

Pl. IX. p. 67.

J. Wands sc.

The Tomb of S.ʳ Henry Crisp and his Lady daughter of Thoˢ. Scott Esq.ʳᵉ

IN THE QUEX CHAPEL, BIRCHINGTON CHURCH

in 1558 had charge of the Kentish coasts committed to his care. At the time of the Reformation, in the reign of Edward VI he was appointed to be one of the Church Goods Commissioners who collected inventories of all church ornaments and furniture in Kent.

He married as his first wife, Katherine Scott of Scott's Hall, Smeeth.

The altar tomb with recumbent stone figures representing Sir Henry and his first wife, Katherine Scott, with Sir Henry in armour and with sword, and the Lady Katherine in the clothes of the period can be seen in the Quex Chapel.

Sir Henry died in 1575.

It was this Sir Henry's grandson, another Sir Henry Crispe, who, as a result of trouble between him and his second wife, Ann Nevinson and her relatives, nearly lost all his estate and it was only recovered by an Act of Parliament in the reign of James I.

The memorial to this Crispe and his father John Crispe, is the famous six-bust monument in the Quex Chapel, a remarkable work of art by the celebrated sculptor, Joshua Marshall, Master Mason to Charles II. This monument to the two Crispes, father and son, each with their two wives, is unique as it is the only one in England with six busts.

On the death of this Sir Henry Crispe in 1647 the estate passed to his elderly cousin, Henry Crispe of Great Chart, who became known in the history of Birchington as Bon Jour Crispe. It was this Henry Crispe who in the year 1657, was kidnapped from Quex by a party of armed men under the leadership of a certain Captain Lendall, taken from his bed, conveyed in his own coach to Gore-end and thence by boat to Bruges in Flanders and there held to ransom for £3000, a very large sum in those days. The story of this kidnapping and the efforts to get his release is told in another part of this book.

Bonjour Crispe and his two wives were buried in the Quex Chapel of Birchington Church, and here will be seen a lovely alabaster monument to Lady Marie Crispe the first wife of Bonjour Crispe, a member of the great Kentish family of Colepeper of Bedgebury, near Goudhurst. This monument showing the kneeling figures of Henry Crispe and his wife Lady Marie with their four sons and one daughter was probably executed by one of the distinguished Johnson brothers, one of whom was the sculptor of the world famous monument to Shakespear in Stratford-on-Avon Church.

The Quex estate continued in the Crispe family till 1680 when, on the death of Thomas Crispe, the property was divided among his four daughters, one of whom was Anna Gertruy Crispe, well known in Birchington history as the founder of the Crispe Charity, which gave rise to the first Charity School in Birchington.

South View of QUEKES, at BIRCHINGTON, THANET.

FROM BIBLIOTHECA TOPOGRAPHICA BRITANNICA — 1787

QUEX 1991
Photograph: Daryl Harding

In 1700 the four co-heiresses, Francesca Wiat, Elizabeth Clapham, Marie Adriana Brenton and Anna Gertruy Crispe, sold the property to John Buller, of Morval, Cornwall and also a merchant of the City of London. The estate included "all that Isle and Building adjoining to the North aisle of the Parish Church of Byrchington aforesaid belonging or appertaining to the said Mansion House of Quex." This of course refers to the Quex Chapel.

In 1718 the estate became the property of Sir Robert Furness of Waldershare.

About 1767, Lord Holland purchased the estate and although he never resided at Quex he may have visited it.

By this time the mansion was showing signs of age and decay, although Lewis in his "History of the Isle of Tenet" says, "it is a large commodious old building partly of brick and partly of timber."

Bibliotheca Topographica Britannica of 1787 says "This ancient seat is fast going to ruin, the weather penetrates into most of the apartments particularly westward of the porch which have been the principal ones, the tiles are blown off in many places, the windows demolished and no part of it inhabited, or indeed fit to be, except a small portion at the end, which is occupied by a farmer."

The following advertisement appeared in the Kentish Gazette in 1769,

"To be let — The Mansion House of Queax, Thanet, with gardens, orchards, stables, & c lately in the occupation of Stephen Elliott. Enquire of Rev. Mr. Willes at St. Peter's Thanet."

During the 18th century a portion of the Quex Mansion was let to farmers. Francis Neame resided in a portion of the house and William Neame followed him.

In 1774 the estate was purchased by John Powell who was Henry Fox's general factotum. When he died in 1783, the estate passed to his sister Elizabeth, wife of William Roberts. Elizabeth Roberts died in 1788 when the estate passed to her husband. At his death in 1805 it fell to the second son, John Roberts, who took his mother's maiden name of Powell and was known as John Powell Powell.

As many parts of the mansion house were in ruins his first act was to pull it down which was completed in the May of 1806.

The new mansion, built a short distance from the old was ready for occupation in 1813 when Squire Powell Powell took up his residence at Quex. It was expected to be completed in two years after it was started but owing to the drain of workmen from Birchington for the Napoleonic War it took much longer than expected. It was enlarged in 1883 when the

Dining Room was added and again in 1904.

The Waterloo Tower with its octagonal turrets and slender openwork spire on flying buttresses, the building of red brick, was built by Squire Powell Powell in 1818, three years after the Battle of Waterloo. The spire forms a landmark for miles around. It houses a peal of 12 bells and there is a tradition that he offered to build a tower at the west end of Birchington Church and to place therein a peal of bells but that his offer was declined, so he built the Bell Tower in the Park. Squire Powell was a great lover of bells and at the Grand Opening of the peal, two Societies of Twelve Bell Ringers of London were invited and rang peals. The bells were cast by Thomas Mears of Whitechapel, one of the only two bellmakers still left in the country to-day. They cost £826 and apart from Canterbury Cathedral this is the only 12 peal in Kent.

Squire Powell also contructed the Sea Tower or Observatory in 1814 as a look-out and signalling station to enable him to contact his friends at sea. Squire Powell was High Sheriff of Kent in 1822 and in honour thereof the name of the old New Inn in Birchington Square was changed to the Powell Arms.

On Squire Powell's death in 1849, the estate passed to his nephew Henry Perry Cotton of Kingsgate. He died in 1881 and was succeeded by his son, Henry Horace Powell Cotton. He died in 1894 and his remains now rest in the Mausoleum in Quex Park which was consecrated by the Bishop of Wakefield in 1897. He was succeeded by his son Percy Horace Gordon Cotton who adopted the name of Powell in conjunction with Cotton. He became famous as an explorer, naturalist and big game hunter and founder of the world wide known Powell Cotton Museum. During the First World War, Quex was opened as a hospital for wounded and invalid soldiers with Mrs. Powell Cotton as Commandant. During the Second World War, Quex was prepared for use as a civilian first aid post but was not required. For a short time in 1940/1941 it was used for makeshift accommodation for soldiers stationed in the Park.

Major Powell Cotton died in 1940 and was succeeded by his son, Christopher Powell Cotton, Esq., C.M.G., M.B.E., M.C., J.P., the present occupier.

Each summer several of the mansion's rooms are open to the public. The Drawing Room is furnished as an Oriental room, the Cotton family having close connections with the East India Company. The furniture is Indian and Chinese, made for European use. In the Hall is a cannon known as Napoleon's Cannon and is thought to have been used by him as a signal gun. It is a English cannon captured by the French near Aboukir in Egypt in 1797. There are a number of relics of Napoleon here also. In the Billiard Room is a beautiful Tudor Fireplace of Kentish

THE 'WELCOME HOME' TO MAJOR AND MRS. POWELL COTTON IN 1907 AFTER THEIR MARRIAGE IN NAIROBI IN 1905
THE 'ARCH OF WELCOME' NEAR THE SQUARE BUILT BY THE BIRCHINGTON FIREMEN

ragstone, ornamented with the arms of the Crispes, the Tudor Rose and various allegorical figures. Originally this fireplace stood in the old mansion. At the top of the stairs is an ancient marble bust, The Laughing Philosopher, given to Lord Holland and later acquired by John Powell. In the mansion are several cabinets of valuable and beautiful porcelain, Chippendale, Japanese and Chinese.

The Powell Cotton Museum, one of the finest outside of London, was founded by the late Major Powell Cotton who devoted some fifty years of his life to the study and collection of Indian and African fauna, ethnography and kindred interests. Later members of the family continued to collect ethnographical material and contributed in other ways to the Museum.

The Museum opened as a single room in 1896, and was added to in 1901, 1928, 1957, 1965 and 1968. The Museum also houses a fine archaeological collection, of material mainly collected in Thanet.

Gallery 8 which houses The Chinese Imperial Porcelain Collection was added in 1973. This gives covered access to the House from the Museum.

The Visitor Centre was added in 1992 which includes a shop, new entrance and new toilet facilities.

The front verandah was enclosed which gives a covered way from the entrance hall to the Museum galleries.

A restaurant was built in 1994.

From 1995 Marriage Ceremonies are able to be conducted in the hall of Quex Mansion.

THE KIDNAPPING OF HENRY CRISPE, ESQ., OF QUEKES

In recent years much has been heard of the kidnapping and holding to ransom for large sums of money of important persons but this is not new. Over 300 years ago on July 18th, 1657 an audacious and daring kidnapping and holding to ransom took place in Birchington. The story of this is certainly a strange one.

On the night of July 18th, 1657 when Oliver Cromwell ruled England as Lord Protector, a party of 40 armed men, under the leadership of a person who called himself Captain Lendall, landed at Gore-end — now Minnis Bay — marched to Quekes, surprised the house and carried away captive the head of the Crispe family, Henry Crispe, Esq., who was nearly 80 years old. He was taken to Gore-end, put on board a ship and carried off to Bruges in Flanders and held to ransom, and there he remained for eight months.

How Captain Lendall carried out this abduction is described in a rare Commonwealth pamphlet and a letter written by the nephew of Henry Crispe, Esq., under the title of "Sad News from Kent".

The following is the nephew, Henry Crispe's account,

SAD NEWS FROM KENT
viz

Shewing how forty armed men, desperate fellows, plundered Sir Nicholas Crispe's house, after which they set a watch over his servants at twelve o'clock at night July 18th, 1657, and carried them to the waterside to be transported to Dunkirke.
With Sir Nicholas Crispe his escape from them upon terms.
Sent in a letter by young Mr. Crispe of Dover to his kinsman in London, Mr. Kathern, who desired the truth might be published to prevent mis-informations.
London, Printed for Richard Harper in Smithfield near to the Hospital Gate 1657
Cousin Kathern,
  My kind love remembered unto you and my cousin your good wife. I know you have heard of that sad news from Queax. There came about forty men well armed with carbine, pistol and sword, and poleax very man there, it is thought they came from Dunkirke, thus coming to the house they quickly

broke the lock of outward gate, so entering into the outward court they secured all the servants lay without the doors, then came to the dwelling house, and knocked very loud, one asking who was there, being about 12 o'clock at night, they told him they must come in, and the party that spake to them but being new laid down in his cloathes, before he could come down with four blows at the hall door, with a two-handed sledge the door gave way and entered the hall before him, secured him and the rest of the servants immediately that lay within the house, then caused the maid to show them my uncles chamber and Sir Nicholases, when they were entered they told them they wanted money and that they well could supply their wants, which was done after three hours time in the plundering the house, and what they could get, they then told my uncle and Sir Nicholas that they must go along with them, and to that purpose carried the coachman to put the horses in the coach to carry their plunder and uncle and Sir Nicholas to the waterside, and on the way had a parlie with Sir Nicholas about leaving him behind, it was agreed immediately that he ingaging to pay them 1000 pounds in 28 days time at Bridge to one they named, that he should be free to come home again, which was done. So Sir Nicholas returned home again, but my old uncle they have inhumanely carried away in his old age, and as yet we hear not any word of the least there of how he doth or where he is. Thomas Smith the butcher went voluntarily along with him. I could not well sooner give you this account, for we knew not the certaine truth of things till my father came home about the middle of last week. My father, wife and self present our kind love unto you. I am sure if he return not speedily we shall want him dearly for he is very good towards my aged parents.

    In haste with thanks for all your favour, I remain,
       Your affectionate kinsman to command,
           HENRY CRISPE.

I pray at your leisure convey this letter to my father in laws Lodging.

In the Public Records Office are a number of documents relating to this abduction, and the efforts made by the Crispe family to secure the release of Henry Crispe, Esq.

Sir Nicholas Crispe, the son of the aged Henry Crispe petitioned Oliver Cromwell the Lord Protector of the Commonwealth to be allowed to exchange certain Spanish prisoners for his father. In this petition to Oliver Cromwell, Sir Nicholas Crispe stated what had happened and that he had been forced to promise payment of £1000 within one month at Flanders, his father being held as security, and also that £2000 has been demanded as ransom, otherwise his father would be "used in strange manner if those moneys be not forthwyth paid and at present keep him from conversing with anyone but in their hearing or writing without their p'usall and apprebacon." Sir Nicholas stated that there were in Chelsea College Spanish prisoners of quality and ability who were willing to go to Bruges to ransom his father. They would go on security to return again within a time limit if they cannot secure the freedom of Henry Crispe. Sir Nicholas asked Oliver Cromwell to give these prisoners leave to go to Flanders to endeavour to arrange his father's release.

Oliver Cromwell granted the petition to allow the prisoners to go to Flanders on security of £3000 and to return if they could not secure the release. One of the prisoners was permitted to go abroad immediately to get the required security, but it seems as if this attempt to obtain the release of Henry Crispe failed.

In the meantime a plot was formed by three men to secure the freedom of Henry Crispe and to gain a reward in lieu of the ransom to be paid to Captain Lendall but Henry Crispe refused to be a party to the plot. The idea was to release him by letting him out of the window of his room but Henry Crispe informed Lendall of the ruse. The details of the plot were given to Henry Crispe and the sum of £1500 was to be given to the plotters for his escape. From the records in the Public Records Office it seems as if at least two of the plotters were examined by one of His Majesty's Secretaries (that is of the exiled King Charles II), so the plot failed. It was no doubt this and other matters that caused Oliver Cromwell and his Council to believe that the whole affair was a ruse to secure money for the exiled King Charles II.

Sir Nicholas Crispe again petitioned the Lord Protector requesting him to allow him to have liberty to negotiate for the ransom with his own money. Captain Lendall wrote to Sir Nicholas accusing him of a breach of promise and of trying to frighten him with Oliver Cromwell. In the September of 1657 the Lord Protector and his Council informed Sir Nicholas that they "refused to permit Crispe to be ransomed, intending no encouragement in attempts of like nature," and also that a trumpeter would be sent to the Commander in Chief of the English Forces in France to inform the Commander of the Spanish Forces that if ill usage continued against Mr. Crispe the like may be expected towards Spanish subjects in England.

Unfortunately Sir Nicholas Crispe died soon after and was buried in the Quex Chapel of Birchington Church in November 1657. The negotiations were continued by his widow, Lady Thomasina Crispe who again petitioned Oliver Cromwell. Just before the death of Sir Nicholas, one of his cousins, John Crispe applied to Oliver Cromwell for permission to go to Flanders to negotiate for the release of his uncle and to try to procure better treatment for him. Lady Thomasina's petition was referred to the Lord Protector's Council who agreed that she could send over a person to Flanders to endeavour to free her father in law from his imprisonment, "by such means as she shall think fit."

It seems as if a Thomas Crispe, nephew of Henry Crispe, Esq., went to Bruges to inform Henry Crispe that in order to raise sufficient money to ransom him some part of his estate must be sold, for which purpose he was authorised to sell or mortgage the estate at Stonar. It is said that Thomas Crispe went six times to Bruges on this business, no light task in those days of travel. At last the money was raised, the ransom paid and Henry Crispe released and returned to Thanet. He had been detained in Flanders for eight months yet he had never been able to acquire the French language further than to pronounce the two syllables, "Bon jour" and for this reason he came to be called on his return from captivity, Bon Jour Crispe.

Henry Crispe, Esq., lived until 1663 but there is no trace of him in the Birchington records except his burial on the 27th July 1663.

In the Burial Register is this entry,

1663 Henry Crispe Esquire was buried July 27.

In the Gentlemen's Magazine of November 1809 appears an article on the kidnapping of Henry Crispe which quotes from "Bibliotheca Topographica Britannica" XLVth Number published in 1787. That article states that Mr. Crispe had been for some time under apprehension of an attack, and loop holes for the discharge of muskets were made in different parts of the house, and he is said to have afforded very generous entertainments to such of his neighbours as would lodge there to defend him.

It is certainly a strange story.

In the present house are preserved in one of the rooms three curious vestiges of this story, three basrelievos, one representing Mr. Crispe in his bed, and another of the mode of his being seized and carried off. They were removed from the old mansion when it was demolished early in the 1800's.

THE ALABASTER MONUMENT TO MARIE CRISPE *(Colepeper)*
*first wife of Henry Crispe, Esq. in the Quex Chapel, Birchington Church
From "The History of the Isle of Tenet" by J. Lewis.*

BIRCHINGTON — PART OF THE MANOR OF MONKTON

SAXON QUEEN EDIVA
and why Monkton supplied Birchington with a Curate or Minister until 1871

The Church of St. Mary Magdalene, Monkton is the mother Church of All Saints, Birchington. Until 1871, just over 100 years ago, Birchington was part of the ecclesiastical parish of Monkton and the Vicar of Monkton was also Vicar of Birchington and also of St. Nicholas at Wode. He had to supply a Curate or Minister to serve the Churches at Birchington and at St. Nicholas at Wood. This dates back to the time when Birchington became part of the Manor of Monkton in the year 961 A.D. The Manor of Monkton was a large manor which extended over most of the western part of the Isle of Thanet, from the lynch or boundary parting it from the lands of Minster Abbey to the Wantsum Channel, excepting the lands held by the monks of Reculver, now forming the parish of St. Nicholas at Wade.

In the year 961 A.D., Queen Ediva, a Saxon Queen, the only child of one Sigelm, an ealderman of Kent, and widow of King Edward the Elder, gave the Manor to the monks of Christ Church, Canterbury. The gift was a thank offering from a pious Queen for the recovery of her lands which she had been unjustly deprived and from that time the parish and manor received the name of Monocstun or Monkyston — the Monks Land.

The Manor consisted of marshland, pasturage, arable land and forest. The woodland seems to have been confined to the centre of the manor — hence we get Wode, afterwards Woodchurch, and Acol or Acholt, a name which seems to imply oak which originally abounded here, the acorns from which would afford pannage or food for the hogs specified in the Domesday Survey.

The Manor of Monkton is described in the Domesday Survey under the general title of Lands of the Monks of the Archbishop, that is Christ Church. This survey known as the Domesday Monachorum is an ancient manuscript preserved in the Cathedral Library at Canterbury. This Survey says that the Archbishop himself held the Manor of Monkton. According to the Survey the area of the arable land was probably well over 3,000 acres, most let to tenants.

The monks did not reside at the Manor but probably resorted there occasionally — probably to recuperate near the sea. It probably made a pleasant change for sick monks to reside for a while in the breezy lands of Thanet. In 1871 Birchington was made a separate Vicarage and Parish

dyve the good queene and noble   other,
o   thelſtane,   Omund,   and ldred,
inges of   ngland: uery each after other:
o hriſtś   hurch, of   anterbury, did giue indeed,
onkerton, & horndenn,   the onkes   there to feede,
epham,   leeus,   owlinge,   fterland,
alt farlengh,   and   enham as   we beeleue;
he yeare,   omo,   LXI   of   hriſts, ncarntion,

15th CENTURY PAINTING OF THE SAXON QUEEN, EDIVA wife of King Edward (the Elder) in the Chapel of St. Martin, Canterbury Cathedral.

from Monkton but the Archbishop of Canterbury still holds the gift of the living.

In Canterbury Cathedral, against the north wall of St. Martin's Chapel in the North Transept is a 15th century painting in oils on a panel 42 inches by 27 inches of the Saxon Queen, Ediva, who died about 970 and whose bones were placed after the rebuilding of the Choir, 1175-1185, on the north side of the altar. At the top of the picture is a village with a church with a spire. Tradition has it that this village near the sea is Birchington. In the picture can be seen a conventional representation of the Manor House of Monkton, and a figure of a man, doubtless intended to represent a forester, an officer who is frequently mentioned in the monastic account rolls.

At the foot of the picture is a scroll with an inscription stating that "Edyve the good queene" ———— "To Christe Church of Canterbury did give indeed, Monketon ———— the monks there to feed."

Monkton is still a small agricultural village whereas Birchington has by far outgrown it and is now a small town.

THE CHURCHES AND CHAPELS OF BIRCHINGTON

The Parish Church of Birchington stands in the centre of the village on a slight eminence adjacent to the triangular Square, and like other churches of Thanet about three quarters of a mile back from the sea. It is at the crossing of two old roads, one which led from Minster Abbey to the sea at the little port of Gore-end, and the other to Canterbury crossing the Wantsum by the ferry at Sarre. Its venerable tower with its tall, graceful spire forms a landmark on the approach to Thanet, and years ago ships passing by on the offing used it as such.

It is believed that a Church stood on this site many years before the present building was erected. It is possible that a Church stood here in Saxon times. The date of the building of the present church and the names of its founders are not known but from the records and from the style of architecture the oldest parts of the Church are the Chancel with its side chapels and the Tower. These belong to the Early English period of architecture and were probably built early in the 13th century. The Nave with its five fine arcades of five bays and two narrow aisles is in the Perpendicular style and dates from the 14th century.

It is possible that the original owners of Quex may have built the original church, specially as the north or Quex Chapel is the private chapel and property of the owners of the Quex Estate.

The walls of the Church are very thick and solid, built of rubble and faced with broken flints, the Kentish cobbles.

The south wall has some old stones incorporated in it which can be seen on either side of the south porch. These old stones which are of anterior date to the other stones used in the building have given rise to the tradition that they were brought from an ancient church which stood at Gore-end and which was pulled down on the encroachment of the sea and used in the re-building or enlargement of the present church.

The Chancel has on each side two Early English arcades rising from plain imposts. The piers, of old Kent Ragstone, are octagonal and have well moulded caps and bases. The east window was rebuilt of Bath stone at the Victorian restoration of the Church in 1863 when the present tracery was inserted.

The south chapel, or the St. Margaret's Chapel, is one of the oldest parts of the Church and over is the Tower occupying an unusual position at the south-east end of the Church. But when the small original church of the three chapels was built in about 1250, before the Nave was added in the early 1300's, the Tower was in the usual position — at the south-west end of the church. The Tower, crowned with an ancient shingled

The Chapel of **All Saints** *Birchington.* 1736

From "THE HISTORY OF THE ISLE OF TENET"
by J. LEWIS

spire is the only ancient shingled spire in Thanet. The spire has been reshingled many times — the last in 1968 with Canadian Red Cedar Wood shingles. In the days of sailing ships the Spire was of great use to ships at sea to steer by on their way from the Thames to the Foreland and Trinity House made a grant of £100 in 1864 to repair it. The Spire is surmounted by a vane in the shape of an arrow with the date 1699 cut out of the vane.

The Nave was probably built in the 14th century. The piers of the arcades are of old Kent Ragstone and at the bases of some of the piers are stone seats which until the end of the 14th century were in most churches the only seats in naves.

Just opposite the south door on the north wall may be seen the outline of an arch used formerly as another door and blocked probably at the restoration of 1863.

For many centuries the Church has had a tiled roof which has been renewed on several occasions. Much of the woodwork of the roof was renewed at the 1863 restoration.

The Chancel is dedicated to All Saints. The beautiful reredos, completed in 1883 takes the form of a triptych and was designed by a Mr. C. N. Beazley and painted by Mr. N. H. J. Westlake, F.S.A., a well known artist at that time. On the north side of the Altar is what is probably an Easter Sepulchre. The oak Altar rails were installed in 1938 and were made by a local craftsman. Attached to a pier on the south side of the Chancel is a brass of a priest wearing the vestments of the period. The brass was formerly on a ledger stone in the Sanctuary. The inscription states that the brass is to John Heynes, priest, sometime vicar of Monkton who died 9th October A.D. 1523.

ALL SAINTS CHURCH, BIRCHINGTON, 1991
Photograph: Joyce Taylor

The theme of the east window is the Crucifixion and was dedicated in 1873. The west window was the gift of Mr. Thomas Gray of Birchington Hall, later to become Spurgeons Homes and then Birch Hill Park and was dedicated in 1873.

The two light window near the font is in memory of Dante Gabriel Rossetti.

The Quex Chapel, originally the Lady Chapel is a private chapel belonging to the owners of the Quex Estate. In the vault beneath the Chapel, now filled in, are buried the previous owners and their relatives of Quex. The Chapel contains some remarkable and interesting monuments in brass, alabaster, stone and marble commemorating the owners of Quex from the early 15th century to the present day.

There are eight bells in the Tower, the oldest being made in 1633. The Church Clock was installed in 1887, as a memorial of Queen Victoria's Jubilee. There are a number of old and interesting tombstones in the Churchyard, the one of most general interest is that of Rossetti whose grave lies near the south porch.

A full account of the Parish Church can be read in "A Guide to the Parish Church of All Saints, Birchington" by Alfred T. Walker and can be obtained at the Church.

THE WESLEYAN METHODIST CHURCH

THE WESLEYAN METHODIST CHURCH

The Wesleyan Methodist Church is situated in the Canterbury Road and was built in 1830. It is of stock brick with a central crenellated clock tower. The other part is also crenellated with three double lancets with tracked heads. It has a simple doorcase having a pointed arch with "Gothic" glazing. The side elevation has three windows.

The clock is probably older than the building as it is believed to have been on the old Margate Pier before being erected on the Methodist Chapel in 1830. In 1902 the clock was put into a state of repair after being silent for two years to commemorate the Coronation of King Edward VII, and the two persons who had much to do with the raising of the money for this were Mr. James Pemble and Mr. George Pointer who had much to do with the turning down of the suggestion to erect a fountain in the Square.

The Chapel was re-dedicated in July 1966, after restoration. In 1976 the clock was repaired by two Naval Officers and a team of Royal Marines who scaled the 60 foot tower to remove the hands from the clock face and restore the clock mechanism.

There was a small Wesleyan Chapel at Acol at the junction of the Minster Road and Plumstone Road, which was opened in 1867. Some years ago it was closed and sold to a local undertaker to become a Chapel of Rest.

PRIMITIVE METHODIST CHAPEL, ALBION ROAD

This was situated on the north side of Albion Road and was part of the Birchington Engineering Works. It was demolished in 1988. It ceased to be a Chapel at the end of the 19th century and was bought by Mrs. Gray of Birchington Hall who granted its use to the School authorities at a pepper corn rent for an Infants School. Before that the Infants School was held at the old Institute in the Square. The Infants School remained in Albion Road until 1926 when the new Infants School was built on the National School site in Park Lane.

THE UNITED REFORMED CHURCH (Congregational) MINNIS BAY

The Bay United Reformed Church dates back to 1885 when a Mr. Arthur Haig, was instrumental in building a small wooden church with a grey slate roof on a piece of land he had bought near to the Coast Guard Station. The timber to build the church came from the wood left over from the construction of the Exhibition Building built by a Mr. Rayden, a London Stockbroker. At first the church was interdenominational and Mr. Haig himself conducted the services. The

THE UNITED REFORMED CHURCH (CONGREGATIONAL), MINNIS BAY

congregation consisted mainly of the Coast Guards and their families, a few farm workers and workers from the nearby brickworks. The Coast Guards kept the church clean and ship-shape.

In 1913 the church joined the Congregational Union and the trusteeship handed to that body. In 1934 the old wooden building was taken down and replaced by the present modern brick building, mainly as a result of the bequest of Mr. Arthur Erlebach, Principal of the Woodford House School in Birchington. The Manse was given by the Erlebach family some years ago.

THE ROMAN CATHOLIC CHURCH OF OUR LADY AND ST. BENEDICT

This church is situated in the Minnis Road, next to the old Malthouse. It started life in the last century as a farm wagon shed. It had three low walls, an iron roof and an open side through which the wagons were backed. In 1908 the open side was closed with wood and corrugated iron, doorways were made and the shed made into a church. Later, some lovely panelling was put inside. In about 1956 it was decided to build a new church by building round the panelling so preserving it. American airmen from Manston Aerodrome did much towards this re-building. When completed the new building was 10 feet higher and nearly twice as long as the old one. A new roof was constructed over the old roof. The farm had given place to a Romanesque Church, lovely in colouring and outline. It was consecrated in 1964. The adjoining hall was built in about 1975.

THE ANGLICAN CHURCH OF ST. THOMAS MINNIS BAY

The land on which this church stands was given by a Mrs. Haidee Kearnes in 1924. The church was built in 1932, the foundation stone was laid with full Masonic honours and ceremony by the Lord Cornwallis. This ceremony was unique in as much as a Moslem took an active part in the Stone Laying ceremony. He was Sir Umar Hayat Tiwana, K.C.I.E., C.B.E., M.V.O., who was the A.D.C. to His Majesty the King and lived in Spencer Road when not on duty in London.

The Church was dedicated by the Bishop of Dover early in 1933.

The building cost £2,804. In addition to the land Mrs. Kearnes gave £2000 towards the cost of the new church.

In 1964 the Kearnes Hall was built mainly as a result of an anonymous donation of £4000.

THE CHURCH OF ST. THOMAS, MINNIS BAY
Built 1932 P.J.L.

THE ANGLICAN CHURCH OF ST. MILDRED, ACOL

The little Church dedicated to St. Mildred was opened and dedicated in 1876 on a site given by a Mrs. Charlotte Rogers who once resided at Minster but at that time was residing at Nice in the south of France. The land was given on trust for the purpose of holding divine service and also for a school for the education of children and adults. The building is in the Gothic style of architecture.

The cost of the building was met by means of donations and collections and mainly through the efforts of the Vicar at that time, Rev. John Alcock. The Foundation Stone was laid by the Dean of Canterbury and the School-Church formerly opened by the Bishop of Dover. The Bishop in his address referred to the old church of St. Nicholas at Wode and to the new church in Acol, "the little place in the oak wood."

The building is constructed of an inside stock brick walling faced externally with stone quoins, stone pilasters and stone buttresses. The panels between the stone work are filled with flint. The cost was about £790.

St. Mildred was one of a family of Saints. St. Mildred lived at Minster and was Abbess of the Nunnery there in Saxon times, succeeding her mother Domneva. In 1969, to preserve the Church, it was necessary to insert a foundation around the base of all the walls, suitably designed to stand the bearing pressure of the soil and the loading of the building above.

In early days the building was used as a School as a Church and as a meeting place for the Parish Meetings.

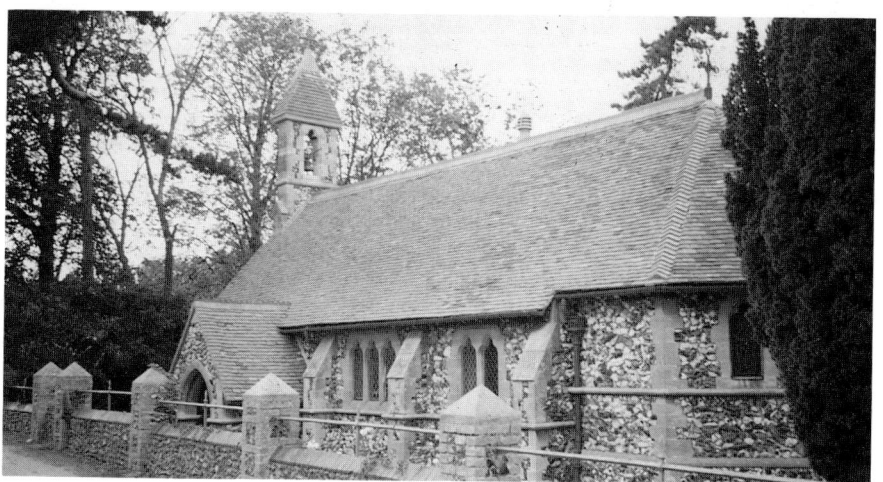

THE CHURCH OF ST. MILDRED, ACOL
Built 1876

P.J.L.

THE BIRCHINGTON BAPTIST CHAPEL
CRESCENT ROAD

The Baptists are first heard of in Birchington in 1740 but their church appeared to have been short lived. They are next heard of as meeting in a little wooden building — a hut — opposite the now demolished Yew Tree House in Canterbury Road. In 1850 the Particular Baptists started their work in Birchington but little is known of them. In 1857 the little wooden building was given up and an iron chapel was used. This iron chapel was in the Canterbury Road at the bottom of Church Hill on the north side. It is marked on the large scale Ordnance Survey Map of 1872. According to the Baptist Association statistics for 1869 the chapel had 26 members with 90 scholars.

For a while the Baptists met in the Cinema Hall in the Station Road and occasionally during the summer, in a tent. Later they met in the old Institute in the Square.

In 1925 the new brick Church was built in Crescent Road on a site given by a Mr. W. H. Cooper, the Secretary of the Church. The old iron building was sold in 1925 and it is now used as a store.

A number of alterations and additions have been made in recent years to the building some being made necessary by the coming of Spurgeons Homes to Birchington bringing so many children into the Church.

In 1971 the Upper Hall of the Church was built.

THE QUAKERS IN BIRCHINGTON

THE MAN WHO WOULD NOT PAY HIS SESS

The very small Quaker community, now known as the Society of Friends, in Birchington and Acol towards the end of the 17th century caused much difficulty and trouble to the village officials at that time.

The Quakers were founded by a George Fox of Leicestershire, who proclaimed that it was in the knowledge that the spirit of Christ was really alive and working in all men, and once this "inward light" was allowed to show them the way, no other guidance was necessary. He proclaimed that priests, ministers, churches and set forms of worship were all unnecessary.

It was at the end of the 17th century and the beginning of the 18th century that this small community in Birchington caused the local parish officials, specially the Churchwardens, such trouble as the entries in the Churchwardens' Book show. They refused to conform like every body else. These people refused to take an oath in the usual form, or to pay their sess or rate, or attend Church like everybody else, or have their children baptised. As a result of their dissent many in some parts of the country were often imprisoned or their estates sequestrated.

The one man in Birchington who caused the parish officials much trouble and whose name appears so often in the records was Elias Hatcher, the sturdy Quaker who fought his battle with the Churchwardens for many years. He refused to pay his sess or attend Church or have his children baptised.

Year after year appears this entry in the records,

"1695 Elias Hatcher, quaker paid noe sess"

"1698 Elisa Hatcher, quaker will noy pay his sess"

In 1697 he was reported for having a child not baptised, like other parents. For November 1697 appears this entry,

"Elias Hatcher had a child born but not baptised."

His father, Thomas Hatcher, was in 1664 presented before the Archdeacon's Court by the Churchwardens for refusing to pay his assessment.

The parish officials became so concerned at the continued refusal and obstinacy of Elias Hatcher that they wrote out in full in their account book the Toleration Act of 1695 by which it was enacted that the solemn affirmation and declaration of Quakers shall be accepted instead of an oath.

The Churchwardens made visits to Canterbury to see the Archdeacon concerning Elias Hatcher, as this entry shows,

> "1699 April ye 15 for my journey to Canterbury to p(re)sent the quaker because he would not pay his Church sess 00 02 06d"

At length the parishioners appointed him an Overseer, responsible for collecting the sess and from that time on there are no more entries of Elias Hatcher not paying his sess. The document recording his appointment was considered so important that it was preserved and it is still in the Parish Archives, signed by the Mayor of Dover, Tho. Broadley.

In the Churchwardens' Book there is the following entry,

> "Medm yt Margarett wife of John Browne was buryed in a new made burying place of the Quakers in the sd p'ish and she was about yt time brought to bed of a girl as yet unbaptised."

It has always been known that there was a Quaker burial place in Birchington but its situation was unknown but tradition has it that it was near the Wesleyan Chapel. In 1966, when workmen were digging the foundations for the additions to the west side of the Chapel, an old grave was found with a much rotted coffin. The plate on the coffin was not decipherable but there is no doubt that this spot was part of the old Quaker burial ground.

There was a Quaker Meeting Place in Birchington and there is every probability that it was at or near Southdown House, next to the Chapel. Southdown House is an old house as proved when extensive alterations were made to the house some years ago. According to the Quakers Quarterly Meeting Book of 1733 to 1753, now in the County Archives Office, it appears that the Meeting House was sold in about 1751.

THE COMING OF THE KING TO QUEX

King William III (1689-1702), who was also ruler of Holland, on several occasions stayed at Quex when waiting to embark at Margate on his numerous visits to Holland.

On occasions the wind was not favourable for sailing so then he would stay at Quex and take up his residence there. At that time it was the property of the heirs of Thomas Crispe, Esq., one of whom was Edwin Wiat, but then in the occupation of John Ball, Gent.

A room said to be the bed chamber of the King used to be shown to visitors before the old mansion was pulled down at the beginning of the 19th century. His guards, so tradition says, encamped in an adjoining enclosure. The beautiful state chair used by his Majesty while at Quex is still preserved at the mansion and is still on show to visitors. This chair was also used by King George IV at Ramsgate on the occasions of his embarkation to and return from Hanover in 1821.

In the Kent Records is a letter written by one of his secretaries while the King was staying at Quex.

This is a copy of the letter,

> 1691 Birchington, near Margate. Sunday 3 May so at night.
>
> This is to acquaint you for the information of their Exlys the Lords Justices that the wind being at S.S.E. His Majesty went on board his Yacht near Margate about two this afternoon but the wind veering to the Eastward in the Evening and then being in appearance of foul Weather His Majesty is returned to this place where he will probably stay until there be a fair Wind. His Majesty is Lodged at Mr. Sergeant Wiat's house in Birchington Parish within 3 miles of Margate.
>
> I am
Sir
Your most humble Servt
Wm Blathwayt
>
> The Duke of Shrewsbury
> went away towards Canterbury
> as soon as ye King went on Board
> and we expect him here again
> tomorrow morning with my
> Lord Rumsey who left at the same time.

The Birchington Churchwardens' Book show how the people of this place welcomed the King by the ringing of the Church bells. It was customary for the Church bells of the parish through which the King or Queen passed, or stayed, to be rung on both entry and departure. The royal almoner claimed the right to levy a fine on the parish for the neglect of this loyal custom, hence the Birchington bells were rung.

Here are extracts from the Churchwarden's Account Book,

1691 Oct the 20th paid the ringers when the King landed at Margate 00 07 06
1695 Spent when the King landed at Margate 00 07 06
1697 March 22nd Paid the Window Newby for beare for the Ringers when the King was here 00 04 10
May 28th Spent on the Ringers when the King come to Quex 00 04 06
1699 Spent on the Kings return from Holland 00 03 00
1699 Spent when the king landed 00 10 00
1699 Spent on the Ringers when the King come home it being also the Kings birthday 00 05 00
1700 Spent on the Kings return from Holland 00 03 00
1693 Novm payed to henary sprakling for bear for the ringers for the kinges retorn from Flanders 00 02 06

The bells were rung on all notable occasions such as Coronations, births of Princes and Princesses, victories on land or sea and celebrations in a truly English fashion, and the ringers were encouraged with a plentiful supply of beer as the accounts show.

THE CAGE, THE STOCKS AND THE WHIPPING POST

Each parish possessed its stocks and whipping-post and also a cage or lock-up for immediate detention. Birchington had all three.

The Constable of the parish was responsible for the repair or reconstruction of these implements of punishments. He was also given the task of whipping of men, women and mere children for such crimes as begging without a licence. After the whipping the vagrant had to receive a small sum, usually 2d, as an aid in proceeding to another parish.

The Stocks, Whipping-post and the Cage were situated, as far as is known, in the Square near the Churchyard wall, when the Square was an open space probably partly grass covered and with no paths as now.

No doubt the whipping post was one of the posts at the end of the stocks, suitable rings being attached for holding the offender's wrists. For almost any offence the stocks could be used. By an Act of Elizabeth I, attending bull baiting or sports on Sunday could put a man in them as did also "profane swearing" in the time of William and Mary. If the culprit was under 16 years of age, he was whipped instead of being put in the stocks.

There are references in the Churchwardens' Accounts Books and in the Poor Books to the stocks and whipping-post.

1606 for pinnes for the Stockes	iiiis iiiid
1648 Paid Robert Covell for staples for the stockes and whipping post	1s 0d
Paid old Coppen for whipping of three vagrants	6d

There are several entries of money spent on whips for the Constable, usually about 4s or 5s.

Unfortunately the accounts of the Deputy, whose responsibility it was to pay for these items are missing except those for the years 1648-1654 - during the Commonwealth period of Oliver Cromwell.

These accounts include amounts paid as above and also are interesting as they include amount spent on the building of a new watch-house and repairing the old costing £4 3s 6d.

Other entries include,

For pitch, rozen and brimestone for the beacon	2s 6d

For mending and cleaning the watch musket	1s 2d
11 bushells of Coals for the Watchmen at 9d the bushell	8s 3d
For an iron bar and hasp to keep Francis Brise from an escape	1s 0d
For sending a vagabond to St. Nicholas	1s 0d

THE CAGE

Birchington, like many parishes, had a Cage or lock-up for the immediate detention of ill behaved and riotous persons. It was the Constable's duty to keep it in repair and for its upkeep. Birchington's cage was a brick building and was not only used for the detention of vagrants, ill-behaved and riotous persons but was also used for storing parish property used for the repairing of the roads by the men who were unemployed.

Often in Birchington, persons apprehended, for example for Bastardy Orders, were kept in one of the local inns for the night until they could be brought before a magistrate at Dover by the Deputy,

It was in December 1787 that the Vestry agreed to build a Cage, as this entry shows,

> Dec. 1787 Agreed to build a Cage at ye end of ye Poor houses to confine ill-behaved riotous persons.

The Poor houses were probably near or adjoining the Churchyard wall on the north side.

In the following year the cage was built at a total cost of £12 12s 0d. The following entries are from the Poor Books,

> 1788 John Friend Senr. paid for bricks & lime for ye cage   £4 11s 9d
> Jn Tipper paid £6 2s 3d his Carpenters bill for the same
> Jn Covell paid £1 18s 0d his blacksmiths bill for the same

John Friend was Churchwarden and also Overseer of the Poor in 1787. He is buried in the Friend vault at the west end of the north aisle of the Church.

About this time, John Tipper did a great deal of work about the Church. In 1774 he re-shingled and repaired the Spire.

In 1828, the Vestry resolved that the Parish Tools, Barrows etc., shall be brought and placed in the Cage every night or such pauper neglecting to comply with this resolution shall be scotted half a days pay.

It seems as if the Cage was used for the storing of coal, probably for the poor receiving out relief.

    1788 for a Lowance when
          delivered out of ye Cage
          25 B (bushels) of Coal   4d

Also when a person was detained in the cage over night a guard was needed.

    1788 Paid Stephen and John Kemp
          for Guard 1 night at ye Cage   3s
    1791 James Garner in the Cage and
          paid for a small blanket for him   6s
    1815-16 To John Friend Deputy
          Birchington to pay ye
          Bills for building at
          the Cage   £24 0s 4½p
    1816-17 Pd Edward Young for
          New Lock and work
          done at ye Cage   £2 6s 1d

In 1831 the Cage was again repaired.

The Cage no longer appears after this date and there is no record of it being demolished.

THE MAYPOLE

Birchington certainly had a Maypole situated in the Square near the Churchyard gate not far from the Inn — then the New Inn.

The Map of Birchington dated 1688, made by a Thomas Hill for a John Bridges, of Canterbury who had purchased Church Hill Farm, distinctly shows the Maypole in the Square, but not known as the Square in those days. The map was really to show the Church Hill Farm and the different parcels of land were coloured. For many years the map hung in the Parish Church until it was stolen in 1957. All that now remains of the farm is the cottages opposite the Churchyard in the Canterbury Road. This map shows the Maypole and a number of other interesting things in Birchington. It shows the pond at the bottom of Church Hill near Court Mount, the Tithe Barn behind the Church, pulled down many years ago and taken to New Barnet to become a Museum, and the Church with the tower at the west end and not at the east end as it should be. It shows the Alehouses in the Square, the Inn adjoining the Churchyard which is now the Powell Arms, but then the New Inn and also the house on the south east side of the Square, which tradition says, was the original Acorn Inn.

There are only two references to the Maypole in the Churchwardens' Accounts Book. They are for the taking down and the setting up of the Maypole.

1606	for the taking down the Maypole	Viiid
1636	towards ye setting up of ye Maypole	6s 8d

There is no doubt that festivities took place near or around the Maypole in the Square at Hocktide, that is on the Monday and Tuesday following Easter and during Whitsuntide and at Mayday. There was a Hocktide Light or candle in the Church and money given for it. Money gathered from these festivities was used by the Churchwardens for the Hocktide light.

THE WAX HOUSE AT BIRCHINGTON

HOW THE CHURCH WAS LIT IN EARLY DAYS

Birchington Parish Church, like other medieaval churches of England, was no doubt lighted in early days artificially in two ways — by lamps and by candles. Up to the so-called Victorian Restoration, there was a gable in the Church roof which let in a little daylight. Old prints of the Church show this gable.

Lighting for practical purposes — that is for worshippers to follow the prayers in print or Mss, or to join in the responses, chants or hymns not known by heart — was quite unknown. Few people at this time could read. The usual offices were said by day-light save at the early winter masses.

Every mass had its own light or lights and the great festivals such as Christmas, Candlemas and Easter had their own special illuminations.

In very early days, no doubt cressets and mortars, which were cups hollowed in stone and filled with grease or oil with a floating wick were used. Later candles were used and their chief use was devotional.

Birchington Church having a number of Altars and Images required so many candles or lights before them that it had its own Wax House where the candles were made, old and new wax mixed and the candles "streeked". "Strekying" is an Old English word for striking or casting or moulding, the candles and tapers. The word is now obsolete — it really means making straight or stretching. This word appears several times in the Churchwardens' Accounts as well as payment made to the "chaundeler", to-day chandler.

The Wax House was a little house on the north side of the Churchyard near the boundary wall to the Inn — now the Powell Arms. It was here that the Lights for the Church were made. St. John's Church in Margate also had a Wax House which was burnt down in 1641.

In the Churchwardens' Accounts dating from 1531 — the time of Henry VIII — are many entries regarding wax, tapers and candles, specially for the period before the Reformation.

From early Wills dating before the time of the Churchwardens' Accounts, it appears that there were several altars and images in the Church each with their own special lights.

In 1402, Hammond de Westgate in Thanet willed to be buried in the Birchington Churchyard and he left 4d to the Light of the Church, 4 bushels of corn to the Light of the Blessed Virgin Mary (that was in the Quex Chapel), 4 bushels of corn to the Light of St. Nicholas (that was probably before the High Altar), 2d to the Light of the Holy Trinity and 2d to the Light of St. Margaret.

Thomas Walter in 1414 left corn to the Lights of the Holy Trinity, St. Anne, St. Mary and St. Margaret.

Richard Queke of Birchington bequeathed barley to the Lights of the Body of Christ and the Holy Trinity, in 1458. He is buried in the vault of the Quex Chapel where there is a brass to his memory.

Laurence Queke of Birchington in 1476 willed to be buried in the Churchyard of Birchington and left barley to every Light in the Church.

In 1472, Stephen Johnson left barley to the Light of Corpus Christi. John Petitt left barley to the Lights of St. Christopher and St. George, and Thomas Wynne in 1500 left barley to the Light of St. George.

There were lamps usually before the High Altar in honour of the reservation of the Blessed Sacrament and except for this lamp, candles in time superseded lamps.

The first entry in the Churchwardens' Accounts is for 3 pints of oil costing 6d. In the following year there are 5 entries for oil,

  1532 Itm for one potte of
    oylle   VIId ob (½p)

In 1534 is this entry,

  1534 Itm for ii lamps   iid

The Wax Chandler is mentioned several times,

  1544 Itm to Thomas Carlow
    (changler) for streykyng
    of the cross lyght &
    Xii li (pound) of Waxe   Viis viid
    Itm payd to Carlowe
    the wax chaundeler
    for XVii tapers XXVi
    pound maed for the
    Rood loft   Xiiis
  1546 to the waxe chaundeler   Viiis

A considerable amount of wax was needed for all the candles and tapers used in the Church. The barley bequeathed to the Church for the Lights was sold by the Churchwardens to buy wax and it appears that the rent of some Church land was paid in wax to make candles.

From the terrier of Church Lands dated 1531

  The Fourth pece contaynit half one akye — and payith be yere a pounde of waxe.

  The XI pece one akyre — and paith be the yere ii li (pound) of waxe.

  Itm ii akyres of land lying at Paynets closse and payith to the kepyng of the pascoll for ewyr to the weight of X li of waxe.

This was probably to supply the great Pascal Taper.

From the Churchwardens' Accounts there appear to be the following Lights in the Church,

> The Cross Light
> The Trinity Light
> The Pascal or Easter taper
> The Hoptyd or Hocktide Light
> Font Tapers
> Candle before the Sacrament
> All Hallows Light (All Saints)
> Christmas Candle
> The Judas Candle

Across the Chancel arch was the Rood Beam — the stone on the north pillar of the arch supporting the rood beam can still be seen. Probably the Cross Light was on the Rood. The Cross Light is mentioned every year from 1531 to the end of reign of Henry VIII that is 1547.

> 1531 Itm for Strekyng of the cross lighte XXV li and a halfe of olde wax, meyt & drynke & streking XVd.
> Itm delividit to Thomas Calowe at Estr in the XX yer of kyng Hary the VIIIth of the churche waxe XVii li qtr (17¼ lbs) Re(ceived) of hym agayne ii tapyrs of Vi li a pyce & ii tapyrs of V li apyce & Viii tapyrs and a tapyr of ii li and a fonte tapyr of a li.
> In newe waxe XV li and iii qtr. s(um)ma for waxe & strekyng iXs Xid.

At Festival times it was customary out of devotion to the Rood to use the front of the Rood beam for the support of a variety of lights — usually on pricket spikes in the midst of bowls of latten or pewter. Also in addition to the row of lights along the beam there was always a special Light, sometimes a lamp and at other times a great candle or taper immediately in front of the rood which burnt either perpetually or at stated times.

The Trinity Light is first mentioned in 1531.

> 1531 Itm for strekyng of the
> trinite lyghte for
> strekyng, meyt & drynke
> and waxd   viiid

The cost of providing ceremonial lights was one of the heaviest of the Church expenses at these times before the Reformation but one which all classes of the community were ready to contribute. The Birchington Churchwardens' Accounts have numerous references to the purchase of wax and the cost of striking or moulding the tapers.

The Pascal Taper which stood by or near the Altar was very large and weighed several pounds. The Church owned 2 acres of land in 1531 which paid 10lb wax a year as rent for the Pascal Taper.

Birchington had a Judas Candle — a kind of 'save all', a wooden stock painted to resemble a candle. It was a sham candle and so named after the sham apostle.

  1555 (Mary) Itm payd for
    makyng of the Judas   iiid

Sometimes the Churchwardens' Accounts open for the year with an account of the wax and tapers handed over by the outgoing Churchwardens. Much of the Churchwarden receipts were spent on wax, streking and tapers.

At the beginning of Queen Elizabeth's I reign the Altars and Images were taken down and so the wax was not needed so much. In 1558 Sir Henry Crispe in return for materials supplied for repairing the Church costing £3 16s 4d, took the wax which weighed 24 lbs.

Candles were used to light the Church until the middle of the 19th century. Brass sconces were used for the pulpit, the Reading desk and on the font. Marks where these were fixed can still be seen.

Gas lighting was introduced in the middle of the last century. A new set of gas fittings was furnished by Mr. Gray of Birchington Hall — later to become Spurgeons Homes. Before these oil lamps were used. Electric light was installed in 1934.

The Wax House was probably converted to a house for the Minister officiating at Birchington in the early 1600's and then demolished in the early 1700's.

HOW THE PLAGUE HIT BIRCHINGTON

Birchington, during its history, has suffered on several occasions from visits of the Plague and epidemics. Some outbreaks of this dreadful pestilence can be traced in the Churchwardens' Accounts Books, the Parish Registers and in the Poor Books. There is no doubt that Birchington had many attacks of plague before records were kept there is no doubt that Birchington was severely attacked by the Black Death in the mid 1300's.

The plague was probably bubonic plague, caused by fleas carried by rats. Like all other places, Birchington had no main drainage, only earth closets and no proper water supply as we have now. All the water came from wells and the remains of these are still in existence near the houses of the original village round the Square. There was no collection of rubbish — it was thrown out into the roadway hence disease spread quickly. In some years, Birchington appears to have been over-run with rats — the spreaders of disease — and it was the duty of the Churchwardens to pay for their destruction. In one year, 4137 rats were killed and paid out ½p per head for their destruction, costing £8 12s 4½p.

The earliest recorded visitation of the plague was in the 16th century and caused the second book of the Register to be called the "black book". The first book of the Register of Birchington ends in 1553 and then follows this entry,

> Here endeth the first boke of the Register of Birchington, The second boke called the blacke boke was spoiled by an ignorant woman.

It was probably called the "black book" because of the many deaths recorded in it due to the plague.

The year 1544, the time of Henry VIII, was a bad year when there were 50 burials when the average was about 12 only, and the population of the place was only about 350 to 400. The visitation lasted from the June to the following March, September and October being the worst months when there were 13 burials in the September and 15 in the October.

In the years 1625 and 1626, the time of James I and Charles I, there was an outbreak of the epidemic which may have been brought to Birchington by a "traveller" or beggar from Canterbury, who died and was buried in the churchyard. His burial is recorded in the Burial Register. In 1625 there were 31 deaths, and in 1626 41, when the average was about 12. Of these 72, many were the breadwinners of the family, in fact 14 and the widows and orphans had to be provided for by the 40 ratepayers of the parish.

The year 1637 was a year when Birchington was again "visited" by "God's heavy hand" when there were 64 burials in this small village. This year is the blackest in Birchington and Acol's history. The Minister here at the time was George Stancombe who remained at his post and buried all 64, all of whose names are recorded in the Burial Register. Of these 64, he wrote the word "plague" against the names of 35. Of these, 14 were breadwinners so the 40 ratepayers had to find quite large sums of money to provide for the widows, orphans and the sick. During this year there were no less than 5 "cesses" or rates levied for "the necessary relief of the poor and visited sick people."

The Overseers of the Poor and the Churchwardens raised, by these 5 cesses, nearly £70, a considerable sum in those days, all of which, with the names of the rate payers, duly recorded in the Account Book. What would ratepayers say to-day if they received 5 rate demands for the relief of the poor in one year!!

The accounts, though simply containing the items of expenditure, form one of the most striking histories of the visitation. They tell of the efforts made to cure the disease, of its infectious nature carrying off whole families, of the method of burial, of help given to widows orphans and the sick.

Here are a few extracts from the Birchington Poor Book for 1637,

It to Dr Randolfe at 2 sevall tymes 5s and to Mr. Watson ye Apothecary at 2 sevall tymes 27s for phisicke for ye visited people and one jronery to Canterbury about ye same business 4s in tote	01 16 00
It to Jo Penny for ye use of his wheelbarrow to carry ye visited dead people for burying	00 02 00
It to Roberts his wife for burning old ragges yt lay about	00 00 06
It to Will Twiman & his wife during ye tyme of there restraint for necessaryes from Aug 2 1637 unto ye 14 following	00 19 0˙

It to Jo Thorpe his wife & children from Sept 6 1637 unto Sept 28 following ye tyme of theire restraint	01 19 00
It to Edw Smith his wife & children from Sept 28 1637 to No 26 following ye tyme of theire restraint	04 04 06ob
It for ½ chauldron of coales ye poor visited people and fetching ym from Margate	00 11 06

Note — a chaldron was an old coal measure holding 36 heaped bushels or 25½ cwts. These extracts are from the Acol, or Ville of Wood Poor Book:

It to Will Derricke from May 7 1637 unto June 11 following 5 weekes at 6d ye weeke	00 02 06
It to him from thence unto Sept 3 following 12 weekes at 1s ye weeke	00 12 00
It to his wife in ye tyme of her sickness extraordinary	00 03 00
It to ye widd Twiman for looking to her one weeke then	00 02 00
It to Nic Hoskins wife for looking to her one weeke then	00 01 00
It for coales for then	00 00 09
It for burying her first child 6 Aug (she was 4 months old)	00 02 06
It for burying her second child Aug 23 (she was 4 mths)	00 02 06
It for burying herselfe Aug 31	00 02 06
It to ye women for watching with her, laying her forth, socking her, & washing her cloathes	00 04 03

It for beere to ye men yt brought to ye church	00 01 00
It for cloathe to make Derrickes other children cloathes	00 08 00

Then follows a number of items for making the clothes, for gloves, stockings, aprons, bodices, neck-cloathes, etc., and for keeping the other children of the family. This gives some idea of what was done in those days to help the sick and distressed.

1644 was another bad year, for the Overseers' record in their Poor Book, "This yeare the parish beeing visited with Godes heavye hande there weare three assessments made and confirmed for the use of the Sicke & poore of Birchington."

From the accounts the following were supplied to the sick and poor,

It a Legge of Mutton	00 02 04
It One joynt of meate Julye 16	00 02 03
It 4 Pounde of Butter & a cheese of 5lb weight	00 02 01
It to Thomas Rogers for 5 gallons of Beanes	00 01 09
It for a Sheete & a Blankett for Goodman Wallis	00 04 06
It to William Seaman for a Sheepe	00 09 06

1669, the time of Charles II, was another bad year when there were 57 deaths in a population of less than 400. Happily Birchington and the Isle of Thanet were free from Plague at the time of the Great Plague of London in 1665. In that year there were only 11 burials so it seems as if the Great Plague did not reach here until nearly 4 years later in 1669. But the people of Birchington did think of the sufferers in London as there were 5 collections here to help these sufferers and it appeared that the people gave generously.

These extracts from the Churchwardens' Account Books show this,

> Mem August ye 2 1665 being ye fast for ye averting of Gods heavy visitation of ye Pestilence there was collected in ye Parish Church of Birchington ye sume of Twenty five shillings.
>
> This is signed by J. Ayling Vic ibid.
>
> William Drayton   John Turner   Churchwardens.

October ye 4th 1665. Collected in ye Parish Church of Birchington for ye relief of ye poor visited people the sume of 1 li 03s 00d.

In November the sume of 12 shillins was collected.

In Dec 1665 Rec. for ye visited of ye Plague nine shillings and sixpence in ye pish of Birchington.

Again in the following January the sum of five shillings was collected "for visited of the Plague".

From an examination of the Registers and the Poor Books there does not seem to be any further outbreaks of epidemics since 1669.

HOW BIRCHINGTON CARED FOR ITS POOR

THE POOR BOOKS — 1611 to 1800

In the Middle Ages, up to the time of the Reformation in the Tudor times, the Church and the Religious Houses were the chief agents of charity for the poor, but when the religious houses were dissolved, in the time of Henry VIII, the problem of dealing with the poor, always acute, became alarming.

As a result, the great Poor Law of Elizabeth I was enacted in 1601 by which each parish was made responsible for its own poor, through its Vestry. In theory, the Vestry was all the ratepayers of the parish, meeting at least once a year, to elect its officials, and to supervise their conduct of affairs. By this Poor Law, the parish was required to appoint Overseers whose duty it was to levy rates for relief of the poor and to assist the Churchwardens in the running of the parish.

The Churchwardens of Birchington and Vill of Wood (Acol), considered the Poor Law of 1601 so important that an extract from the Law was written in their Account Book. So, once a year, the Vestry elected these unpaid parish officials, the Churchwardens, the Overseers of the Poor and later, the Surveyors of the Highways, and when it is considered that a great deal of what now-a-days is done by the District Council, was done in the 17th and 18th centuries by a few unpaid local men, it cannot but be realised that they must have been of outstanding qualities. Some could not even read or write so quite often the Minister at Birchington kept the accounts and the officials made their marks against their names and the Minister was then paid for so doing.

The Churchwardens and Overseers, with the consent of the Vestry, levied cesses or rates, relieved the poor, apprenticed poor and orphan children, built Poor Houses and did what they could to find work for the unemployed.

Their accounts were kept at first, on single sheets of paper and then in books, which became known as the Poor Books. In Birchington there are a number of single sheets and 8 Poor Books, dating from 1611 to 1840, except for the period 1676 to 1738 which are missing. The single sheets and the first 4 Poor Books have been transcribed and typed out. These accounts, with the Churchwardens' Accounts give an enormous amount of information of what Birchington was like during these times. No other parish in Thanet has in its archives, Poor Books and Churchwardens' Accounts as Birchington has. Acol, or the Vill of Wood as it was known, appointed its own Overseers and kept its own Poor Books which are still in existence.

These parish officials were elected annually on Easter Monday, usually at 12 noon, when the accounts were approved and signed — or marks made. The Chairman of the Vestry was always the Minister.

The Vestry was called the Vestry, as originally it met in the vestry of the Church, but usually its first act was to adjourn to the local hostelry — now called the Powell Arms — but referred to in the accounts by the name of the innkeeper — Mays, Dads, Blews. Here they had refreshments which were paid for out of the cess and the amount spent duly entered in the Poor Book. The office of Churchwarden or Overseer was rarely held for more than two years but occasionally one man held two offices.

Birchington's earliest account is on a loose sheet of paper for the year 1611 when Vincent Underdown was one of the Overseers. A few years later, in 1619 and 1620, he was one of the Churchwardens. His total receipts came to £4 11s 4d from 22 ratepayers, and his "layings out" came to £4 19s 4d to some 12 widows and elderly people, but mainly to Widow Durant and to Tho. Dray. The population of Birchington in 1611 was about 300. Of the 22 ratepayers, Sir Henry Crispe of Quex paid £1 6s 2d and the lowest amount paid was 5d.

The account of Robert Cavill Overseer for 1613, written on a loose sheet of paper, is interesting. The number of ratepayers was 30 contributing a total of £8 7s 11d. The highest amount paid was £1 12s and the lowest 3d by a Thomas Kemp. Tho. Kemp became Overseer in 1614 and 1615. Robert Cavill paid 3s 10d for a "sheete & buriall" for Widow Seas. No coffins were used then. In this account appear the old English words of "bodge" and "tovet".

3 bodges of wheat were given to Freemans widow at a cost of 3s. A bodge was a quarter of a bushell or a peck.

4 poor people received a tovet of wheat each costing 2s a tovet. A tovet was 2 pecks.

In 1615 appears the first of a series of assessments set out in detail, for the relief of the poor. It includes a list of holders of land, the acreage and amount of cess paid. There were then 36 ratepayers. Sir Henry Crispe, of Quex and Robt Seath together had 234 acres for which they paid 19s 6d. There was also a charge on "revennues", sometimes called "ability". In 1615/16 Sir Henry Crispe paid £1 5s 0d for "his revennues". The lowest amount paid was 2d. The total receipts came to £9 15s 0d and the cess is signed by the two Churchwardens, Richard R. Gilberd and Arnold Pepy, who made his mark, also by the two Overseers, Thomas Kempe and Thomas Crumpe.

In 1616-1617, two assessments were made each at 1d "ye acre" and "ye revennues at a peny in ye pound". Again there were 36 ratepayers.

The total collected from the two assessments came to £20 3s 6d ob (ob = ½d). Of this sum, much went to widows of Birchington at about 1s a week and just over £10 was paid out for the keeping, clothing and apprenticing the children of Henry Arthur who died in 1616. He married an Amy Cooper in 1596 and they had 7 children 4 of whom died when quite young. The Overseers paid for the burial of Henry Arthur — for "socking" — that is wrapping the corpse in its grave clothes and to sew the body in its winding sheet. The 3 children were boarded out with widows costing 1s, 1s 6d and 1s 8d respectively a week. One child, Catherine, was apprenticed to Robert Crump who was the Parish Clerk for 5 years. Robert Crump received £2 10s. He was to "informe, instruct, teach and traine up ye said Catherine — in ye best manner he can", and he was to clothe and feed her.

Valentine Arthur, another child was apprenticed to Thomas Coulner in 1621, who agreed to teach him the "art of husbandry". He was apprenticed until he was 24. These indentures are in the Parish Archives. There are 82 indentures in the archives, all drawn up by the Overseers and signed by the Mayor of Dover.

From these Overseers accounts, for the keeping of the Arthur children, the cost of articles of clothing and what clothes were worn can be ascertained.

> A pair of shoes for Catherine cost 1s 6d.
> A pair of hose for Catherine cost 1s 6d.
> The boy aged 6 wore a petticoat costing for making 4d.
> Margaret's shoes cost 1s 6d.
> Her "smocke" took an ell and a qtr of canvas and cost 1s 8d.

An ell is a measure of length originally taken from the arm — and was probably 1¼ yards.

The boy wore a "trusse" or tight drawers or breeches, may be worn under the breeches and made of canvas.

Margaret needed 4 yards of russet to make a "petticoate and wastcoate" at 2s 3d ye yard. Russet was a course homespun cloth. Margaret also had 2 "coyfes" or close fitting caps.

Quite often the Overseers bought corn and then sold it to the poor at a much lower price. In 1622, the Overseers bought over 5 seams of barley for the poor at 26s per seam and sold it to the poor for 1s 6d per bushel. A seam was 8 bushels.

In 1624, the Overseers paid for "a winding sheete for a poore vagabond boy, for socking him and for his buryall 5s 8d."

Also "for a winding sheete for a poore wayfaring man, one Ralph Bibbin 2s 6d."

This poor wayfaring man is alleged to have brought the plague to Birchington. In 1637, the year of the plague, when there were 65 burials, 14 of whom were house-holders and the bread winners, the Overseers levied 5 sesses.

The accounts for the years 1653 to 1665 are rather pathetic as much of these accounts refer to the Widows Thorp Senior and Junior. Both received 6d per week and occasionally they were given a little extra for looking after other old people. In 1658, Widow Thorpe Junior was given 3s for looking after old Knight and his wife and later received 5s for tending him in harvest. Widow Thorpe had a lame daughter and special shoes were bought for her costing 3s and occasionally a special shoe was bought for her lame foot costing 2s. In 1666, Widow Thorpe Junior died leaving her daughter to the care of the Overseers which duty they carried out. The expenses of the funeral are set out in the Poor Book.

1667 Paid Charles Alaby for a knell an grave and going to Mounton (Monkton) for the Minester to bury the Widow Tharp	0 5s 0d
Paid George Smith for a Coffen for the Widdow Tharp	0 7s 0d
Paid for Biere	0 6s 0d
Paid for bering of her to the Minester	0 1s 0d
Paid more for laiing of her forth	0 2s 6d
Paid Robert Kennet for thinges and sume fagotes to burne to wash the linen	0 5s 7d
Paid Frannes Brise locking to the Widdow Tharp in her sicknes and for washing the linen	0 7s 0d

Having buried the poor Widdow Tharp the Overseers, or Collectors, then proceeded to sell her goods to help recuperate some of the money given to her while she was alive. A copy of the goods sold is in the Poor Book and it gives a good idea of what the home of an ordinary person was like. She had been a widow for 14 years and had inherited her mother's home. It seems to have been quite a comfortable home with good beds, useful utensils, two spinning wheels and a fair quantity of linen.

A Copey of Widdow Tharpes goodes that the Collecteres sould.

1667 It one fether beed one fether boulster, to fether pillwes, one whit blanckit, to cuffarlides	£3 17s 0d
It one pine bedsted, one truckel bedsted and one mat	1 3 0
It one flock bed, one flock boulster and one cuffarilid, one whit blanckit	0 8 0
It one skout and one cubbard	0 9 0
It one iron poot	0 3 4
It one iron poot	0 2 2
It one washing block to kelenes for	0 1 0
It one bras skilet and a warming pan	0 1 6

Note — a skillet was a small metal pot with a long handle and usually had legs used for cooking.

It one linen whelle and one barrell	0 2 6
It one paire of pot hangers one brine tub	0 3 6
It one mat and a litell ladle	0 2 6
It one chest and a forme	0 1 8
It one chaire and one wolen whele, a salte box and to keler	0 2 6
It one wastcot sould for	0 2 6
It one paile sould for	0 1 0
It one pelle sould for	0 1 0
Which comes the sume of	£7 2s 2d

Soon after a "wastcote and a cote" were bought for Ann Tharp — the lame girl, for 16s.

There are several references to payments to the doctor and to a nurse for their services. In 1671, £1 10s was paid to Doctor Samson for setting Elizabeth Fisher's leg, and a nurse was paid 2s for curing "Lawrances" leg. A Dr. Silver was paid for inoculating the poor people for cow pox.

Weekly allowances continued to be given to the deserving poor all through the 1700's, and some poor were housed in the Poor's House by the Churchyard Wall from about 1670. The allowances were any amount from 1s to 4s per week. When there was famine or when bread was very dear, labouring men were allowed to have rough meal at a much reduced price and better off people were urged not to eat bread so as to leave more for the poor.

There are a number of entries stating that money had been given to applicants with begging letters or briefs, and to soldiers returning home after serving over seas. In 1630, 6d was given to 2 poor maimed soldiers, and in 1687, 6d was given to a poor slave whose tongue was cut out. Again in 1663, 4s was given to a poor woman which had the King's patent to ask and receive, they being fourteen in family.

In the second half of the 1700's some parish children were sent to St. Peter's where there was a workhouse, the Overseers and Churchwardens paying the cost.

Looking back over the preceding centuries the poor of Birchington had always been comparatively well off. Certain chronically poor families are traceable all through the period. They were tolerated and assisted. But reformers were at work and in 1834, new legislation began to sweep away the old Poor Law and the Union Workhouse was built.

THE BIRCHINGTON WORKHOUSE, THE POOR'S HOUSE, THE ALMSHOUSES

Birchington has always done its best to relieve the poor of the parish, the widows, the aged, the disabled, and the orphans. The amount of time, attention and money spent upon matters relating to the poor seems to have been quite as great as that devoted to all other matters of local concern together. In 1601 was passed the great Poor Law of Queen Elizabeth I, and this act formed the very foundation of local poor law administration for over two centuries.

The most important sections of this act ordered the Churchwardens and four, three or two substantial householders to be nominated each year as Overseers of the Poor, imposing on them the duty of maintaining and setting to work the poor, the funds being provided by taxation "every inhabitant — and every occupier of lands, houses, —." So begins the Assessments for the Poor as recorded in Poor Books of Birchington and also those of the Vill of Wood, or Acol.

At first, the poor were relieved in their homes and were given "out relief". In about 1670, a few of the poor were housed in what became known as the Poor's House. This was probably the Minister's house which had not been lived in since Mr. George Stancombe who was Minister here until he died in 1647, and had fallen into some disrepair. In 1670, it was agreed by the parishioners to make an assessment of 4d the acre and employ half the money so raised in repairing and rebuilding of the Poor's house by the Churchyard. This entry is signed by Tho. Crispe of Quex and Jo. Ayling, the Minister. In the Poor Book is also this entry,

> Burtchington
> Jul the 16th 1670
> A sess made by the Churtchwardens and collectores for the poore and other inhabitants confariming the reprationes of the parish house where the poore doe live at 3 pence the Acre and by Abillite.
> Total collected 24   9s 5d

These Poor Houses were in the north east part of the Churchyard by the wall. In the Poor Book, the accounts kept by the Overseers and Churchwardens for the repair are set out, for the year 1670.

for Timber about the poore house	0	2	6
for John Harty for worke about the poor house	0	1	10

for goodman Hilles for worke aboute the poore house and Timbar had of goodman Hilles	3	2	5
paid to Christo Coulner for beere for the workemen about house	0	3	1

A few years later, in 1675 the Poor's house needed some repair and an oven was installed.

for the oven in the parish house and for Brickes	0	4	10
for the mason one daies worke	0	2	0
more for Irone for the ovenes mouth	0	1	1ob (½)

There is no record of who lived in these houses.

During the 1700's some repairs were carried out to these poor houses and in 1761, 200 tiles were bought for them at a cost of 4s 8d.

In 1810, it was decided to take down the Parish Houses. After a survey, it was agreed to take them down and build them elsewhere on a piece of land near Andrews Cottages, and to repair the churchyard wall. In 1811, 1375 of the tiles were sold to the Churchwardens by the Overseers at 3s 6d per hundred for the repairing of the roof of the Church. Where Andrews Cottages were situated is not known but probably they may have been near the old almshouses.

The old almshouses were situated in Gas Row, adjoining Park Lane. They consisted of one building divided into four single apartments, with heavily thatched roofs and brick walls. They were owned by the Church and up to 1925, were occupied by elderly people. The last to live there was Mrs. Sayer who was aged ninety years when she left to live with her daughter in Margate. She had been living in the almshouses for thirty years.

It is not certain when the almshouses were built but the following extract from the Churchwardens' Account Book suggests that they were built soon after 1810.

> At a meeting of both parishes it was decided to pull down the row of Poor Houses by the Churchyard and to rebuild them elsewhere, the Overseers to find flints and bricks to rebuild the Churchyard wall and the Churchwardens to find mortar and labour.

The houses were vested in the Vicar and Churchwardens. They were condemned by the Old Eastry Rural District Council in 1925 as unfit

THE OLD ALMSHOUSES, GAS ROW
Demolished 1934

for habitation and were demolished in 1934. The Church sold the site for £50 in 1946. The site is now occupied by a garage.

It was in 1761 that "The Workhouse" made its appearance. In 1722/3 an Act was passed which stated that the Overseers and Churchwardens with the consent of the majority of the inhabitants of the parish might purchase or hire buildings and contract with any person for lodging, keeping, maintaining and employing the poor. After some years this is what Birchington did.

In 1761, the Churchwardens and Overseers of Birchington made a contract and agreement with the Churchwardens and Overseers of St. Peter's for the poor of Birchington to be provided for in the Workhouse at St. Peter's. From this time until the time that Birchington had its own Workhouse, poor children and others were sent to St. Peter's Workhouse and in the Birchington Poor Books are entries for payments made for sending the poor to St. Peter's and for the charges of keeping them there.

Here are some entries from the Poor Book relating to St. Peter's, Thanet.

1761 Mary Pinters sent to St. Peters — charges	£3 1s 2d
1762/3 Thos Gore children at St. Peters at 4s per week	
1763 The Overseers charged for making several visits to St. Peters where children were kept. It came to	0 16s 6d
1763 Pd for the keeping of Gores children at St. Peters	£5 5s 6d
1766 For my journey to St. Peters to pay Widow Batchells charges	0 2s 0d
The charges came to	£3 3s 6d

In 1794, Birchington built its own Workhouse. It was established under what is known as Gilbert's Act of 1781/2, the time of George III. Gilbert was a member of Parliament for Lichfield and had a genuine concern and love of the poor. His act was an adoptive one requiring the consent of two thirds of the ratepayers in number and value. This was obtained in Birchington, the Vill of Wood, Monkton and the Vill of Sarr, when these parishes united for carrying out the provisions of the act. The establishment in which the poor were to be maintained was to be a

OUTSIDE THE OLD ALMSHOUSES

Poorhouse and not a Workhouse where the sick, the infirm, aged and young children were to be its occupants.

An Agreement was signed 20th May 1794 uniting these four parishes according to this act, to purchase a piece of land in Birchington and to erect buildings thereon for the reception and accommodation of the poor etc. This agreement was signed by James Neame, who farmed Street Farm and Gilbert Stringer who was the Master of the Charity School and Parish Officer and became the treasurer of this Union Workhouse. The Churchwardens of Birchington, Mr. John Friend of Birchington Hall and Thomas Simmonds, conveyed one half acre of land to the guardians of the poor for the sum of £18. This piece of land was in Park Lane adjoining the present school site. The total cost of the building and furnishing came to £600 which included the brickwork, tiling and chimneys, for digging a well, and a cellar, and for furnishings such as frying pan, pails, fire ranges, spinning wheel, pewter dishes and a bell. The amount was raised by means of loans at 4½% from local 7 prominent people. These included the Stringers and Friends. Soon after it was built, it was enlarged mainly to accommodate the poor of Monkton and Sarr at a cost of £300.

The building seemed to consist of,
> a small garret with beds,
> a long garret with beds,
> a men's room with beds and chests,
> a women's room with beds,
> the Mistress's room,
> at least one other small room,
> a kitchen,
> a cellar,
> a garden.

There appeared to be at least 30 beds, chests of drawers, kneeding trough, carpenter's bench, boiler, warming pan, chairs and tables. There were a Bible and spelling books for the children. The house was insured with the Sun Fire Office for £1 9s 6d per year.

The first Governess was a Mrs. Wootton who was paid a salary of £21 per year. There were two "necessary" houses which were bought at the Camp, situated at Minnis Bay. Looms and spinning wheels were bought and a weaver engaged to teach the inmates weaving and spinning. The weaver was a Peter Petts who was paid 6s per week.

The food given was, according to our standards, very poor. The cost varied according to the cost of wheat and the numbers in the Workhouse. At the end of the 1700's and the beginning of the 1800's, wheat was scarce and costly, in fact there was a famine and well to do people were urged not to eat wheat so as to leave more for poor people.

In 1810, there were 20 poor people in the Workhouse and the cost of "victualling" these for 5 weeks was £14 3s 0d.

The next year, when one of the inmates died, all the others had a little beer — no doubt to cheer them up.

The cost of running the Workhouse for the year 1816/17, for victualling, clothing, salaries and interest on the loans came to £290 5s 10d. It appears that those able were given work to do, the girls were paid for their spinning and weaving, and the men often sent out to repair the roads.

In 1822, an Edward Young agreed to victual, lodge, wash and clothe the poor in the Workhouse and to find them every necessary for 2s 6d per week. At the time there were 31 in the Workhouse.

This is the diet he supplied and agreed to by the Overseers,

Diet	Breakfast	Dinner	Supper
Sunday	Spoon victuals	Meat	Spoon victuals
Monday	do or Butter	Suet pudding	do or Butter
Tuesday	do or do	Meat	do or do
Wednesday	do or do	Suet pudding	do occasionally
Thursday	do or do	Meat or Suet pudding	do or do
Friday	Broth or butter	Soup	Broth or butter
Saturday		not given in the Poor Book	

This arrangement lasted for several years.

In 1808, the Master of the Wingham Workhouse was paid for carriage of materials, iron and woodwork for rope making, and iron work and wood work for the rope making purchased. Often spinning wheels were purchased — in 1813, 6 were bought at Canterbury for 10s 6d each.

It was not always easy to obtain the services of a suitable Governor. In 1819, after an advertisement and after several candidates were interviewed, a William Philmer was appointed.

In 1822, the children in the house were given a total of 4s in lieu of a Christmas present and a Richard Dawson was paid 2s 6d for teaching the children. Later he was paid 10s per year for instructing the children. At this time the only school in the village was the Crispe Charity School, taking about 24 children. In 1834 the Workhouse was closed on the building of the Union Workhouse at Minster now known as Hill House Hospital. Two years later it was agreed to sell the building and effects and the Poor Law Commissioners dissolved the Union of Birchington, Wood, Monkton and Sarr. The building and land were sold to John

Powell Powell, Esq., of Quex for £225. The conveyance shows that there were 1 rood 38 perches of land, The building is now used as a cottage and barn. The documents relating to all the above are in the Birchington records.

The following extract from The Margate Guide Book for 1796 is interesting,

> Near the village of Birchington has lately been erected a very neat and comfortable building for the poor of Monkton, Sarre, Birchington and Acole, here while the helpless infant is cherished and the feeble and aged cottager supported, those who are able to work are employed in such useful occupations as are best suited to their different abilities. A weaver is retained in the house who manufactures coarse sheets and the management of the poor is conducted with such regularity and decency as reflects the highest credit upon the promoters of this very laudable and useful Institution.

SOME OLD TAXES OF BIRCHINGTON

The old taxes of Birchington, specially the Chimney Tax or Hearth Tax, are interesting and give some information as to the number of houses in the village at the time. A Chimney or Hearth Tax was levied in the time of King Charles II in 1662 when every "house, chamber, and lodging was charged with two shillings yearly to be paid at Lady Day and Michaelmas for every firehearth and stove therein".

The Collectors were to collect the tax six days after it was due, and to pay it to the Deputy after deducting two pence in the pound for collecting, and the Deputy paid it to Dover.

The assessment of 1662 gives a complete list of those who paid in the Parish of Birchington together with the number of hearths. There were 78 dwellings listed and the names of 72 who paid the tax, there being 5 empty houses, 27 people who were receiving Poor Relief were omitted. From the list there were 230 hearths.

Thomas Crispe, Esq., of Quex had the largest number of hearths — 17 with 6 in his farmhouse. John Hayward must have had quite a large house as he had 12 hearths and John Curling had 7.

A Samuel Hardwicke was the Collector and George Ruck the Deputy.

In the Churchwardens' Account Book is a list of 25 persons who were excused the tax in 1671, 9 of whom were widows.

In 1673-4, when the population of the village was about 400, 230 hearths were paid for by the occupants of 79 houses.

The total number of hearths in Thanet in 1673/4 was as follows,

	hearths	houses	excused
St. Johns (Margate)	552	174	100
St. Peters	393	168	42
West Boro', St. Lawrence	253	100	107
Ramsgate	234	92	73
Birchington	230	79	27
Minster	221	76	8
St. Nicholas	94	34	4
Monkton	90	31	3
Sarre	47	17	—
All Saints Shuarts	30	7	—
	2134	778	364

The following are taken from the Churchwardens' Account Book,

1672 for riting a note for the chimny man   6d

1674 July ye 6 day paid for a
man to goe to Dover with
a noat of the fire harth   2s 10d

The Act was a most unpopular Act and was repealed in 1689.

Six years after the repeal of the Chimney Tax another tax was introduced, the Window Tax, in 1695. The tax survived until 1851.

By this tax, every house was taxed 3s, except cottages, and every window taxed if the number was above 9. As a result, in some places bricked up windows can be seen. The Parish Official had to count the windows from outside and might only enter a house to pass through it if necessary to count those in the back.

The following references to this tax are in the Churchwardens' Account Books,

1699	for writeing of the Window Taxesses	00 09s 00d
	paid for writeing of Two Taxes one for windows and one for marriages, births and burialls	00 08s 00d
1700	for makeing a window Tax	00 04s 00d
1708	paid the Messenger for bringing of the window tax	00 01 06d
1711	paid the Surveyor of the windows for making of the sess	00 13s 00d

In 1694, another Act was passed to raise money for carrying on the war against France with vigour, which imposed taxes for five burials, marriages and births, and also on bachelors and widowers giving right of access to the Registers. The general tax was for burials 4s, births 2s, marriages 2s 6d, for bachelors and widowers 1s annually with heavy super taxes for the nobility.

From the churchwardens' Account Book,

1699	April ye 15 paid for writeing two sesses of Marriages, birth, and Burialles	00 10s 00d

Another tax, more objectionable than the other taxes was the Poll Tax, levied in 1666. By this tax, every private person was assessed at a shilling, an esquire £10, gradually rising to very high sums for the nobility.

In the Churchwardens' Account are the following entries referring to this tax,

                1699 for writeing of one whole poll tax and two Quarterly polls   00 05s 00

VERMIN AND ITS DESTRUCTION IN THE VILL OF BIRCHINGTON

Just over 200 years ago, over 4,000 rats were killed in Birchington, their tails cut off and counted and ½d paid for each tail. The responsibility for the keeping down of vermin in the parish was that of the Churchwardens. From 1533, in the time of Henry VIII, it was one of their duties and remained so until about 1835.

In the Churchwardens' Account Books there are numerous entries of money paid out for the destruction of vermin, and from these entries we learn not only of the money paid out but also of the kind of vermin destroyed — some of which are no longer seen in this area or even considered vermin, in fact some of which are now preserved and protected.

In 1533, an Act was passed ordering by implication that the churchwardens were to provide the parish with a net for the destruction of "rooks, crows and choughs" and that two pence was to be paid for every twelve old crows, rooks or choughs. A chough is a kind of red-legged crow.

In the time of Queen Elizabeth I, the Act was renewed and the Wardens were to assess holders of land or tithe for the destruction of "Noyfull Fowles and Vermin" and to furnish a fund for paying a penny for every three heads of old "Crowes, Chowes, Pyes or Rooks" and a penny for every six young owls, and a penny for every six unbroken eggs. The heads of the animals and the eggs of birds were to be shown to the Wardens and then cut asunder or otherwise destroyed. This Act was renewed in 1572 and in 1597/8.

In Birchington and Acol, the Churchwardens discharged this duty and quite large sums were paid out for the destruction of the vermin, as the Account Books show.

The first mention by the Churchwardens of a payment for the killing of vermin is in 1673 — the time of King Charles II when sixpence was paid for the killing of a "poullcatt". Over the years a number of "pouldcatts, poulcatts, poulcates, powellcats, poultcats" were accounted for, as well as dozens and dozens of sparrows.

In one year a total of £15 2s 4½d was paid out for 1,700 dozen old and young sparrow heads and it was the duty of the Churchwardens to count these heads no matter how distasteful the task. Although in some years a prodigious number of sparrows were destroyed this did not appear to decrease the supply the next year.

Hedgehogs were considered vermin and a large number were destroyed and paid for.

In some years, Birchington seems to have been over-run with rats. In 1773, the large number of 4,137 rats were killed and ½d per head was paid out costing £8 12s 4½d. This large number is not really surprising when it is considered that at this time Birchington and Acol had no drainage or piped water, and all garbage, rubbish etc., was thrown out of the house into the roadway or on to a heap in the garden where rats flourished. And the roadways, such as they were, were never swept. No wonder Birchington occasionally suffered from a plague and epidemics.

Foxes, rooks and "whezells" were also caught and destroyed as were "baggers" and "puttises". A puttise was probably a stoat.

Sparrowhawks, kites, snakes have all been killed and paid for in the parish. Some of these are no longer seen in the parish or even in Thanet.

Every year, up to 1835, the Churchwardens paid out quite large sums for the destruction of vermin specially rats and sparrows. In 1732, 384 dozen of sparrows were killed as well as 42 hedgehogs and 11 polecats.

It appears that no mention is made in the Accounts for foxes, probably because these were hunted and so the killing of foxes by the ordinary people was discouraged. The Hunt often met in Birchington Square and the Boxing Day Meet in the Square was an event which attracted a large following from all over Thanet and East Kent.

THE AGRICULTURAL RIOTS OF 1830

BIRCHINGTON AND ACOL MEN AND A WOMAN SENTENCED TO BE TRANSPORTED

In 1830, Birchington was still an agricultural village with a population of about 800 living in about 150 houses, including the Coast Guards of the St. Nicholas Station. When the first census was taken in 1801, there were 537 people in the place, living in 100 houses, so the population had not grown much in the 30 years. Most of the men of the place worked on the land for a wage, a little more than two shillings a day. There was considerable unemployment at this period and as a result the poor rate was high, paid by no more than 60 rate payers. The cost of food was high, specially wheat and bread.

In 1829-30, there were four sesses or rates for the poor, bringing in a total of £959 12s 6½d, a very considerable sum for those days. Of this sum, £167 was given out in weekly pensions to widows and unemployed. The Workhouse cost £284 18s 2½d for the year when the number of inmates totalled 28 to 37. Some of the unemployed men were given work on the roads at rates of 1s 2d to 1s 6d per day, picking up stones from the fields to fill the pot holes in the roads.

In 1831-32, there were four sesses bringing in a total of £844 4s 2d to help relieve the poor. Twenty-nine persons received weekly pensions from 1st 6d to 2s 6d per week and the number of paupers in the Birchington Workhouse was 27 to 32. In the 1820's, the Overseers of the Poor paid a man who had a wife, 8s a week for work on the road, with one child, he was given 6d extra per week. If he had three children he had 10s and 10s 6d for four children, per week. The Overseers decided in 1834 that if a man keeps a dog, or ass, or a horse he shall receive no relief.

This state of affairs for agricultural labourers was general in counties south of the Thames, and in the winter of 1830, a few months before introduction of the great Reform Bill, the desperate field labourers marched about in a riotous manner demanding a wage of a half a crown a day, but high rents paid by the tenant farmers and the tithe, made payment difficult.

Farm machinery was broken, specially threshing machines newly introduced and there were also incendiary fires. There were fires at Birchington as well as at other places in East Kent. Threshing machines were broken at Alland Grange (by Manston Airfield). To make matters worse, the winter of 1829-30 was particularly severe and food was dear. The introduction of the threshing machine was resented as it caused unemployment among farm workers as by their introduction, threshing was no longer done by the flail during the winter months, when often that was the only work available. Not only was farm machinery smashed but ricks were burnt. These riots became known as the Swing Riots but who Capt. Swing was is not known.

There were fires at Birchngton in the November of 1830 and threshing machines were smashed at Margate, Minster, Shuarts, Alland Grange and at Chambers Wall. At Alland Grange George Hannam had two threshing machines smashed by men with faces blackened with soot. A few Birchington and Acol men, one from Monkton and one from St. John's, Margate were convicted of "unlawfully maliciously and feloniously breaking a certain threshing machine in November 1830 in the Parish of St. John's, Margate to the value of ten pounds the property of Hills Rowe, farmer of Margate" and were ordered to be transported for seven years. Hills Rowe farmed Vincent Farm. The Birchington man was Richard Oliphant, aged 25, a butcher who neither read nor write and had no trade. He was not married. He was baptised in Birchington Church. His parents were well known Birchington butchers. The Acol men were William Brown who had six children, and William Hughes, age 21, who was not married. Brown could neither read nor write and Hughes could read only. Brown was married in Birchington Church in 1819 to a Sarah Miles and all their six children were baptised in Birchington Church. Hughes was baptised in Birchington Church according to the Baptism Register. A third man who had connections with Acol was Thomas Hepburn, alias Heborn, who was probably born in the parish of St. Lawrence but was married in Birchington Church where the Marriage Register describes him as of Acol. He has two children both of whom were baptised in Birchington. A Stephen Bushell of Monkton aged 28 and William Bushell of St. John's, Margate age 17, were also convicted and sentenced.

They were all tried at the General Sessions of the Peace at Dover and convicted. They were sent to the prison hulk at Gosport and then transported to Van Diemans Land, now known as Tasmania on the convict ship "Eliza" which left Portsmouth on 2nd February 1831 arriving at Hobart, Tasmania the following May. On board were 224 convicts, all of whom were allocated to various settlers to work.

Hepburn was granted a free pardon in 1836 and his wife and children later joined him in Tasmania. His descendants are still living in Australia. All the above were described by the prison as peaceable and quiet. To us the sentence appears to be very harsh.

A Birchington woman also became involved in these riots. She was Elizabeth Studham, the daughter of George and Mary Studham who was baptised in Birchington Church on the 5th April 1814. She took part in the riots and helped to set fire to an East Kent Workhouse. She was brought to trial and sentenced to transportation to Van Diemans Land. On the outward journey she was well behaved and orderly, so the ship's register says, although she was supposed to be of loose habits. In Tasmania she was sentenced for 10 offences mainly for bad language but two for theft for which she received two years hard labour. Elizabeth Studham sailed on the convict ship "May" which docked at Hobart on the 19th October 1831. She was given a conditional pardon in 1846 and was then entitled to move freely in the colony. What happened to her later is not known.

From the Birchington Poor Book it is known that a new plough belonging to Thomas Sidders of Birchington was smashed during these riots. The Overseers of the Poor paid for the repair as shown by this entry:

"1830-31 To Thos Sidders for a new plough butt
in pieces by mischievous persons as p bill
— £3 8s 0d"

Many others from the south of England were sentenced to transportation as convicts and three were even hanged.

Elizabeth, the wife of Thomas Hepburn received outdoor relief from the Overseers of the Poor for the Ville of Wood (Acol) until she and

STATION ROAD — 1913
Opposite the old Woodford House school
The four girls are: Elaine Miles (Walker), Eileen Setterfield (Walker), Katie Hedge and Vera Holton

THE SQUARE — early 1900s — looking towards Margate. Note the horse drawn brakes drawn up by the Queens Head Inn.
On the south side is Hinkleys Stores, later to become Vyes, then a Betting shop and grocers. On the north side the old Verger's cottage, now the Sweet Market and the Post Office.

her children re-joined Thomas Hepburn in Tasmania were a further three children were born. She died in 1854. Thomas died in 1879 at his daughter's residence in Geelong, Australia when he was described as a "gentleman".

The opening of the South Eastern Railway to Margate in 1846, and the London, Chatham and Dover Railway to Birchington in 1863 started the village on a course of prosperity never before equalled and instead

STATION ROAD taken from The Square end about 1910.

of being an agricultural village dependent entirely upon the rise and fall of the value of wheat etc., it became a suburb of London. The change came slowly but many new houses were built, many on the north side of the railway station where bungalows were built. Nevertheless there was still a certain amount of poverty among a few and to help these poor a Soup Kitchen was started, mainly by a Mr. B. Rayden, who collected subscriptions and dispensed soup on two days a week. Soup and bread cost ½d and men had a quart of soup in a jug and bread for 1d.

THE BIRCHINGTON SCHOOLS

Birchington, being such a healthy seaside place, had several schools up to the outbreak of the Second World War but being in a danger area some were evacuated and some never returned or closed after the cessation of hostilities.

THE CRISPE CHARITY SCHOOL

The earliest school and the first school in Birchington of which there is a record was the Charity School established under the Will of Anna Gertruy Crispe, who died 23rd March 1707. She bequeathed in her Will to the Overseers of the Poor of Birchington and the Ville of Acol, 47 acres of land lying in the parishes of Birchington and Monkton — now known as the Crispe Farm — then let at 18 pounds yearly, the income from which, "to keep at school with an able Dame or Schoolmaster the number of twelve boys and girls to be taught and learn to read and to write and the girls to work needlework, to be educated in good manners and to be at Church orderly, and having learned to read to give each at leaving the School, a Bible." So was started in 1709 the Crispe Charity School. It was one of hundreds founded all over England during the reigns of William and Mary, and of Queen Anne. They were very much needed as the State at that time did nothing for the education of the poor, and ordinary parishes such as Birchington had no sort of endowed school although perhaps a village dame taught a few village people their letters in return for a small fee.

Mistress Anna Gertruy Crispe was the last of the Crispes to live at Quex. She was buried in the vault of the Quex Chapel of the Birchington Parish Church where there is a white marble monument with bust to her, on which is inscribed the portion of her Will by which she left the 47 acres of land in trust for the founding of a school, and for poor widows. The monument is by a brilliant sculptor, William Palmer of London.

The first "Dame" was Elinor Jarvis, who was paid December 31st 1709 the sum of £2 11s 8d. In the following March, on Lady Day, she was paid for teaching 12 scholars £5 1s 10d and 10s 6d was paid for 3 Bibles, to give to scholars leaving school.

Where this school was situated is not certain, but it is known that much later the school was situated in a small house at the corner of Park Road and Canterbury Road. Elinor Jarvis was followed by Elenor Huse as

"Dame" in 1715, who remained until 1730. Elizabeth Mirriams succeeded her and remained Schoolmistress for 43 years until 1774, and the most she ever received a year was £10 17s 4d. She was followed by the best known of the Schoolmasters, Gilbert Stringer who was, as stated on his tombstone at the east end of the Churchyard, "33 years Master of the Charity School (the gift of Anna Gertrude Crispe formerly of Quex), Thirty seven years perpetual Parish Officer, Treasurer of the Union Workhouse Thirty Years." Although he was such an important official in the parish his salary until 1810 was never more than £10 a year. Later it was increased to £36 15s 0d a year.

It was Gilbert Stringer, Master of the Birchington Charity School who gave evidence to the Commissioners on Education of the Poor at the House of Commons. He said there was an endowed school at Birchington, that he taught 12 boys and girls and 12 taken in addition, reading, writing and arithmetic. There was no allowance for books and stationery — the parents fund these themselves. He said he built the school room which belonged to him. The 12 scholars and the 12 add lately are always filled up and there are always candidates for a vacancy. The children attended Church regularly. He added that in the Parish of Birchington and Ville of Acole, about 180 children had not the means of education, about 140 of whom attended regularly at the Sunday School. The population at this time was about 700.

After the death of Gilbert Stringer in 1832, the Governors of the Charity School had to face a number of problems, mainly through the lack of accommodation for the increased number of scholars, and the doubts arising as to the ability and efficiency of the Schoolmasters. One Schoolmaster, a Mr. Thomas Sidders, was sent to St. Lawrence School, Ramsgate, "to make himself efficient Master upon the present system of Education." Thay system was the Monitorial System, popular at the time. Unfortunately, the Vicar of the Parish and the Church officials were at variance with the Governors of the Charity School over the establishment of a National School for Birchington. Eventually the Charity School was closed when the National School became well established in 1862. In that year the Governors agreed to an Order of the Court of Chancery by which they were to pay £50 per annum, out of the funds of the Charity, to the National School provided that the children of Dissenters from the Church of England need not learn the Church catechism or be instructed in any distinctive principles of the Church of England, or attend the School or the Parish Church on Sundays.

The Governors of the Charity paid to the National School Managers an annual sum, until 1956, two thirds of the nett annual income.

THE OLD NATIONAL SCHOOLS IN PARK LANE
Built and opened 1848

THE NATIONAL SCHOOLS

The National School, now known as the Birchington Church of England, (Controlled) Primary School is situated in Park Lane. The site was given by John Powell Powell Esquire, of Quex to the Vicar of Monkton, Birchington and Acol, the Rev. Richard Peter Whish, to be used as a site for a school for poor persons of the parishes of Birchington and Acol, and as a residence of the Schoolmaster or Schoolmistress. The original building cost £625, the money being raised by means of subscriptions, a Government Grant, a grant from the Diocesan Board and a grant from the National Society for the Promoting Religious Education in accordance with the Principles of the Church of England.

After much opposition, mainly from the Governors of the Crispe Charity and from a number of parishioners the school was opened on June 11th 1849, with about 60 pupils, boys and girls. The building was pseudo Gothic in style, rectangular in shape about 48 feet by 22 feet, single storey, of local brick with a tiled roof. Attached to it on the north side was the School House of two storeys and next to that the offices. The roof timbers were open to the school room and the floor boarded. The cloakroom was in the porch. At first the school room was heated by an open fire and later by a stove standing out in the room. The playground was in the front of the building, up to the Acol road. The site was surrounded by a rough brick wall capped by flints so common in old Birchington.

The first Schoolmaster was a Mr. A. H. Ansell with Mrs. Ansell as the Schoolmistress, but after a number of years, both were given notice to quit, "owing to the current reports in the neighbourhood as to seriously impair his authority and usefulness and injure the character of the school." The next Schoolmaster was Mr. William Lockyer Banks who was paid £50 per annum and free residence. From now on so much of the information regarding the School comes from the long series of Log Books kept at the school. They are a record of the daily life of the School and in these books the Head Teachers enter accounts of any important happenings, events, visits etc. And what a mine of information they are on the life of the school, the people of the village and local events. A full account of these is now kept at the present school.

Mr. Banks was followed by a Mr. Williams and then by a Mr. Goodbourn when the number on the register was 100. In 1872, a Mr. Herbert Catford was appointed to the mixed school, when the school reached a high degree of perfection.

In 1872, as a result of the Elementary Education Act, the school was enlarged and another room was built on the south side of the original schoolroom and again in 1881, further additions were made to accommodate the increasing numbers.

In 1889, Mr. Alfred W. G. Score became School Master and in 1900 he was succeeded by Mr. C. Laming. Owing to the increasing numbers — the roll was now 247 although the attendance was poor — a new Girls' School was built in 1902 on land situated behind the old school. A Grand Bazaar and Fete was held in Quex Park in order to raise money for this new school, under most distinguished patronage. In 1926 the need arose for a new Infants School, so a third building was constructed on the site — three schools with three separate Head Teachers.

In 1935, with the extension of the boundaries of the Borough of Margate to include Birchington, the schools were transferred from the Kent County Council to the Margate Borough Council. Soon after the schools of the Borough were re-organised and Birchington C. of E. Schools became a Junior Mixed and Infants School, under one Head Teacher — the senior pupils being transferred to King Ethelbert Secondary Modern School, along the Margate Road.

In 1940, at the beginning of the Second World War, all State Schools in Thanet were closed and the children evacuated to Staffordshire — the Birchington children or rather those whose parents wished it, went to Fazeley. As a number of children were not evacuated and as there were no official schools in Birchington, the Vicar of Birchington, Canon N. M. G. Sharp with the help of volunteers, opened the school in Park Lane as a private school and it became known as the "Vicar's School". This Vicar's School continued until the school re-opened in 1942.

In 1972 the old school building was demolished the Girls' and Infants' renovated and the present 'Open Plan' school built.

THE INFANTS SCHOOL IN THE SQUARE

The Trustees of the Crispe Charity established in 1869 an Infants School in the premises adjoining the Institute, behind the Verger's house. This lasted until 1892.

THE INFANTS SCHOOL IN ALBION ROAD

In 1892, Mrs. Gray of Birchington Hall, later to become Spurgeons Homes, purchased the Primitive Methodist Chapel in Albion Road and leased it to the Vicar and Churchwardens for a pepper corn rent of one shilling a year to be used as an Infants School. The back of the room was raised to form tiers and a small piece of land at the side formed the playground. This was used as an Infants School until 1926 when the new Infants School was built on the site of the National School in Park Lane. The Chapel and the adjoining Birchington Engineering Works were demolished in 1988, the site cleared and developed, and flats and houses built.

THE PRIMITIVE METHODIST CHAPEL, ALBION ROAD
THE INFANTS SCHOOL, 1892 to 1926

WOODFORD HOUSE SCHOOL, BIRCHINGTON
Situated in Station Road

WOODFORD HOUSE SCHOOL

Woodford House School was situated in Station Road with the playing field extending through to Albion Road. In 1892, Messrs. A. and H. A. Erlebach, coming from a school at Woodford, Essex, acquired premises known as the Kent County School in Birchington and joining up with the boys of the Kent County School, formed the Woodford House School. The School quickly established itself and the Erlebacks took an active part in the affairs of the village, specially with the Congregational Churches at Westgate and at Birchington. Mr. A. Hodges married Miss Winifred Erlebach, the Headmaster's daughter and later joined the staff as Co-Principal. Originally the school was a boys private boarding school taking up to 40 boarders and a few day boys.

In 1924, Mr. Erlebach presented to the village the "Memorial Ground", a sports and recreation ground in memory of his three sons who gave their lives in the First World War, and three years later, Captain Cornwallis later Lord Cornwallis, unveiled photographs in the pavilion of Mr. and Mrs. Erlebach and the three sons of whom the ground stands in memory. A lych gate was erected to the memory of Mr. Erlebach, after his death and when the school was closed and demolished, it was re-erected at the gate leading to the Parish Church.

Mr. Albert Hodges, the Headmaster, did much for Birchington. He was Chairman of the last Parish Council before Birchington was absorbed by Margate. He was a keen Scouter and Superintendant of the St. John's Ambulance Brigade.

Woodford House School was the only school to remain open in Thanet during Second World War. During the two wars, girls were accepted as pupils.

On the retirement of Mr. Hodges, the school passed to a Mr. Ashley and then to a Mr. Bickerstaff and it was he who sold the premises to a development company who demolished the buildings and built Woodford Court and the shops in Station Road.

GRENHAM HOUSE PREPARATORY BOYS' SCHOOL

This was a well known Boys Preparatory School taking up to about 80 boarders and a few day boys. It was founded by Mr. B. V. C. Ransome, J.P., M.A., and Mr. H. E. Jeston, M.A., in a house at Minnis Bay and in 1910 moved to the building in Grenham Road, which they had built. The school was well equipped with a Chapel, a swimming pool and an extensive playing field. The school was demolished in 1987 and converted into Homebirch House. The playing field into Hunting Gate Estate.

The last Headmaster was Mr. Denys Jeston, M.A.

QUEEN BERTHA'S SCHOOL

This girls' public school in the Canterbury Road was founded by Miss C. M. Hunt and Miss E. Randall Harris in 1929, when they acquired a house called Fernleigh, once the home of Ald. Robert Grant, J.P., C.C., who was the man who gave Birchington its fountain in the Square, in memory of his wife. Later the two principals acquired the adjacent property known as Rosebank, once the home of Lord and Lady Forrester, at that time a boys' preparatory school known as Birchington House School. The school achieved a very high standard, specially in music and drama. The school uniform colours, of gold and scarlet were most distinctive.

On the retirement of the Principals the premises and grounds were sold in 1959 for the residential development and is now Queen Bertha Estate.

SEA POINT PRIVATE SCHOOL

This was a small school for boys and girls up to about the age of 8 years, situated in Sea Point House in Berkeley Road. It was first established in Mildmay, in Epple Bay Road, in the 1920's, then moved to Elfin Cottage in Station Approach and then to Sea Point. Miss Pearson was the Principal. The school closed on the outbreak of the Second World War.

HOME SCHOOL FOR GIRLS, PORTPOOL, SPENCER ROAD

This was a boarding and day school for girls ages from about 7 to 17 years, the Principal being Miss Barnes. It was opened in the early years of this century and closed in about 1935. Gwynant, in Shakespeare Road, was used as part of the school. On the retirement of Miss Barnes, the old Beresford Hotel took over the premises and it became known as Spencer House.

BIRCHINGTON HOUSE SCHOOL FOR BOYS

This was a preparatory school for boys, situated in the Canterbury Road in a house known as Rosebank, once the home of Lord and Lady Forrester. It was opened after the First World War, the Principal being Mr. Sydney G. West, M.A. It ws closed in about 1934 when the Principals of Queen Bertha's School purchased the property and it became part of that school.

KING ETHELBERT SECONDARY MODERN SCHOOL

This school was built in 1938 when the schools of the Borough of Margate were re-organised taking the senior pupils from Birchington, Westgate and the surrounding villages. It has been enlarged several times. It was closed during the Second World War when the pupils were evacuated to Staffordshire.

A group of pupils at the old School in Park Lane in about 1898. This photograph was taken when the School had Boys and Girls, Mixed. Do you recognise any?

1935 Birchington C. of E. Boys School Athletic Champions at the Thanet Schools Sports held at Broadstairs. Photograph taken at Park Lane School with the Championship cups. Do you recognise any?

THE STORY OF THE CHURCH CLOCK

Margate has its Jubilee Clock Tower, erected in 1887, to commemorate Queen Victoria's Golden Jubilee. Birchington, too, has its Jubilee Clock, the Clock in the Church Tower, installed in 1887, as part of the village celebrations of that great event.

The people of Birchington had been anxious to have a Clock in the church Tower for many years, and in 1812 an estimate was obtained for the supplying and fixing of a two dial clock, 5 feet in diameter, in the Church Tower for £131, but probably because of what was considered the high cost, the estimate was not accepted.

Some 36 years later, in 1848, Squire Powell Powell of Quex, offered a clock for the parish if the parishioners would pay for its erection. So a meeting of parishioners was held in October 1848 to consider placing a clock in the Church Tower and the "general expenses thereof". The Rev. Whish, the then Vicar of Monkton and Birchington, offered to contribute £20 towards the fixing of the clock if the parishioners would "do" the remainder of their own expense and would also pay the expense of repair after the expiration of one year.

The meeting accepted the gift and the Churchwardens were instructed to prepare "a respectful letter to Mr. Powell expressing to him their grateful thanks of the Parish for his gift."

Some three weeks later, on November 2nd 1848, another meeting of the parishioners was held "to take into consideration the propriety of a vote, of a vote of thanks to J. Powell, Esq., for his liberal offer of a clock for the Church, and also to rescind a resolution passed at the last meeting." At this meeting it was resolved, "That this meeting is sensible that Mr. Powell is making the offer of a clock for the Church is actuated purely by motives of liberality to the Parish and with a view of benefiting its inhabitants, Resolved that this meeting, taking into consideration the present high parochial rates chargeable upon this parish think it would be imprudent on the part of the Parishioners to accept of any gift that would add to the present parochial burdens. Resolved that the Churchwardens be requested to convey to Mr. Powell the sincere thanks of this Meeting for his kind and liberal offer and although from the above motives they are induced to decline it, they are equally obliged to him for making the offer." It is very curious that the offer was declined by the very same persons, mover and seconder excepted, who voted for its acceptance only some three weeks previously.

The thanks of the meeting were given to Mr. John Wilson, Churchwarden, "for the satisfactory manner in which he had conducted the subject of the day's meeting." All of the above is written in beautiful copper plate hand writing in the Churchwardens' Book.

Mr. Powell Powell was duly notified of the decision of the meeting and he replied immediately for the copy of his reply is beautifully written in the Churchwardens' Book. This is it,

>Sir,
>
>I beg you will convey to the Inhabitants of Birchington my acknowledgement for the dutiful and grateful way in which they have tendered to me their thanks and to assure them I am truly aware from the statement contained in their address the propriety of their declining my offer of a Clock for the Church.
>
>And am
>Sir
>Yours Truly
>J. P. Powell.
>
>Quex Park
>3rd November 1848.

The loss of this clock to the parish was probably owing to two opposing elements which existed in the Parish at that time, also no doubt, to the high Poor Rate at that time to maintain the many unemployed and poor. The above clock was afterwards placed in the turret at Quex.

It was not until nearly 40 years later, in 1887 was a Church Clock again discussed at a Vestry Meeting. In that year it was agreed at the Vestry Meeting to commemorate the Queen's Jubilee by,

1. Restoring the Church Spire and Placing a Clock in the Tower, Provide a Lightning Conductor to the Spire.
2. Rehang the present 5 bells and adding a 6th together with a framework for 2 more.

A Church Tower Jubilee Fund was started and a list of Subscribers appeared in Keble's — now the Isle of Thanet Gazette — Major Morrison Bell gave £110 15s 0d for the Clock, its cost. Mrs. Gray of Birchington Hall, later Spurgeons Homes, gave £100 for the Tower restoration. The Church Tower was duly restored, the bells recast and rehung, the spire reshingled and the Clock installed.

The clock was manufactured by Messrs. Lund and Blockley. The iron guilt dial facing east is 5 feet in diameter and chimes the Westminster quarters on the 2nd, 3rd, 4th and 6th bells. It strikes the hours on the 6th tenor bell which weighs about 13 cwt. All the bearings and hammerwork are of gun metal throughout, built powerfully to resist the great pressure occasionally received during storms on the exposed hands.

It was formally set going by the Rev. J. P. Alcock, the first Vicar of Birchington after separation from Monkton, in September 1887.

In 1958, at the restoration of the Church, the bells were taken down and recast and the Clock overhauled and the face regilded.

In 1968, when the Spire was reshingled, the clock was again regilded with 22 carat gold leaf.

The Thanet district Council now maintain the clock, keep it in repair and rewind it every week.

GABRIEL CHARLES DANTE ROSSETTI AND BIRCHINGTON

Many people who come to Birchington every year visit the Parish Church to see the grave of Rossetti who is buried in the Churchyard and to see the window erected to his memory.

Gabriel Charles Dante Rossetti, a poet and painter, was born in London in 1828. His father was born in Vaslo, Italy, in 1783 and became the Keeper of the Naples Museum. He left Italy in 1821 and came to England and was appointed Professor of Italian Languages at Kings College, London.

Rossetti was one of the founders of the Pre-Raphaelite Brotherhood, a group of artists formed in London in 1848 having for its object the cultivation of the methods and spirit of the early Italian, the Pre-Raphael painters. The group originally consisted of Holman Hunt, Millais and Rossetti. Ford Madox Brown, Ruskin and William Morris were also in the group later. They aimed at producing work in the spirit that prevailed before the time of Raphael.

Rossetti came to Birchington on 4th February 1882, a very sick man, having lived much of his life in Chelsea. In 1881, his health rapidly deteriorated, mainly due to drink and drugs, so he spent the last few weeks of his life in the bungalow — later known as Rossetti Bungalow — situated between Beach Avenue and Rossetti Road, loaned to him by his friend, John P. Seddon, the architect, who designed and built the Bungalow Hotel. The bungalow was quite large and mainly boarded.

Rossetti's friends thought that his health would improve if he moved to the seaside. Mr. Hall Caine, the author, came with him to Birchington. In his book, "Recollections of Rossetti", Hall Caine says, "Birchington was not a holiday resort in those days, it was merely an old fashioned Kentish settlement on the edge of a hungry coast. The village stood back from the shore the better part of a mile, consisting of a quaint old Gothic Church, grey and green, a winding street, a few shops and a wind mill, while the bungalow we were going to live in stood alone on the bare fields to the seaward side." Hall Caine goes on to say, "The land around was flat and featureless, unbroken by a tree or a bush and one felt as if the great sea in front, rising up to the horizon in a vast round hill, dominated and threatened to submerge it." He also mentions that a telescope was installed at the bungalow, and through it they could see Reculver. It is now impossible to do this because houses and high rise flats have been built between the site of the bungalow and the cliff top. When Rossetti and Hall Caine stayed in the bungalow they had a clear view of the sea from the veranda, there was nothing between the bungalow and the cliff

THE ROSSETTI BUNGALOW

THE INTERIOR OF THE ROSSETTI BUNGALOW
Rossetti's Study

top. Often Rossetti stood on the cliffs by what is now known as the Beresford, looking seaward.

During the short time Rossetti stayed in Birchington he was visited by several of his friends including Mr. Frederick Shields, who designed the memorial window in the Parish Church.

Early in the March of 1882, Rossetti's mother, then not far off 82 years old, and Christina, his sister, then 52, went to Birchington to be with him. His brother William also was with him from time to time up to the last.

Rossetti died on Easter Sunday, 9th April 1882.

He was buried in Birchington Churchyard very near to the south door of the Church. It was William Rossetti's decision that he should be buried in Birchington Churchyard and not with his wife in Highgate Cemetery.

An account of the funeral appeared in Keble's Gazette — now the Isle of Thanet Gazette — on 22nd April 1882. The account is as follows,

> The remains of Mr. Dante Gabriel Rossetti, poet and painter, were on Friday afternoon quietly and without ceremony interred in the Churchyard here. At half past three the cortage consisting of the hearse and five ordinary mourning coaches left the sea-side cottage where Mr. Rossetti had been staying during the past six weeks in company with his old friend, Mr. Hall Caine. The deceased was followed to his grave by his mother, his sister, Miss Christina Rossetti, his brother, Mr. William Rossetti, Mrs. W. M. Rossetti, Mr. Theodore Watts, Mr. Hall Caine and others. It had at first been intended to have a public funeral at Highgate where his wife and father were interred but for family reasons this idea was abandoned. At the Churchyard wicket, the procession was met by the Vicar, the Rev. J. Alcock, and the coffin, which was covered with flowers, was carried along the pathway to the Church. It was of polished oak with brass fittings and bore the inscription, "Dante Gabriel Rossetti, born at London, May 12 1828, died at Birchington-on-Sea, April 9, 1882." The Burial Service was read by the Vicar after which the coffin covered with flowers was lowered into the grave. At the time of his death, Mr. Rossetti was engaged on a study of 'Joan of Arc'.

TOMB OF DANTE GABRIEL ROSSETTI
Painter and Poet
(Died at Birchington-on-Sea, 9th April, 1882)

The Grave is marked by a most striking white sandstone monument in the form of an ancient Irish Cross, the arms and stem being connected by a circle. It was designed by his friend Ford Maddox Brown.

At the point of intersection of the Cross is represented the temptation in the Garden of Eden showing the Tree of Knowledge of Good and Evil with the serpent. The upper part of the serpent takes the form of a woman. Below shows the spiritual marriage of Dane and Beatrice. On the stem of the Cross is represented St. Luke, the patron saint of painters and above, the Ox, the emblem of the Evangelist.

The inscription reads,

> Here sleeps
> Gabriel Charles Dante Rossetti
> honoured under the name of
> Dante Gabriel Rossetti
> Among painters as a painter
> and among poets as a poet
> Born in London
> of parentage mainly Italian 12th May 1828
> Died at Birchington 9th April 1882.

His brother William wrote this inscription. On the rear of the monument is,

> This cruciform monument
> bespoken by Dante Rossetti's mother
> was designed by his life long friend
> Ford Madox Brown
> executed by his brother William
> and Sister Christina Rossetti.

In 1893, a letter appeared in the "Morning Post" complaining that the grave was neglected and suggested that an iron railing be put round it. The vicar of Birchington at that time, Rev. John Kirkham Fox, replied saying that the sexton constantly received protests from Rossetti's female devotees because the poet was buried outside the church and abuse from others for allowing Rossetti to have been buried at Birchington at all. The Vicar then received letters from Rossetti's brother and sister who complained about the state of the grave. Eventually an iron railing was put round the grave. In 1900 more letters appeared in the "Times" about the monument's decaying condition but its decaying condition is inexplicable as today the condition is remarkably good and the carving is not blurred or defaced and there is no evidence that the monument has ever been renewed or restored. The stone has been cleaned by a stone mason in recent years.

ROSSETTI'S WINDOW IN THE CHURCH

After Rossetti's death in 1882, Christina and her mother spent 9 weeks in Birchington awaiting the completion of the stained glass window to his memory — to be placed in the Church at his mother's expense. The window was erected to the west of the south door of the Church. All correspondence involved in the design and erection of the window was undertaken by Christina.

The left light of the window is a reproduction of Rossetti's own painting of the Passover and represents the two families of Joseph and of Zacharias uniting to keep the Feast of the Passover. Christina describes the window thus,

> Our Lord holds th basin of blood from which the lintel is being struck with hyssop by Zacharias. One side post has already been struck close to Christ's head. His foot is being shod by St. John Baptist kneeling, allusive to "I am not worthy to stoop down and unloose —". The Blessed Virgin culls bitter herbs for the Paschal Supper for which Joseph in the background brings the lamb, being met by St. Elizabeth. Our Lord is turned in the direction of a dove settled on brickwork near a table on which stand the vessels for supper. A vine grows up the house. A few forget-me-nots grow beside a well with a bucket drawing water.

The bitter herbs being culled by the Blessed Virgin Mary are endives — chosen because it was pictorially beautiful amongst several of the bitter herbs in question. A little bird's nest with eggs can be seen over the head of Zacharias. At the top of the light is Rossetti's monogram, and under is the Biblical reference Exodus Chap XII Ver 35.

The right light of the window was designed by Mr. Frederick Shields, Rossetti's friend and represents Jesus healing the blind man outside the gates of Bethsaida.

In a letter to Christina, Mr. Shields describes the window thus,

> The moment is after our Lord has first touched the blind man's eyes and questions him if he sees ought — I desired in him to express the eager longing awakened by the partial gift of sight for perfect vision. Out of the city the Lord leads him upward — under the low arched street. Pharisee and Disciple, the disciple attracted to the Lord — the Rabbi — warning him not to he led after a false Prophet — above his head, a camel — "ye blind guides that strain at a gnat and swallow a camel."

By the side of the gate growling at the passing Saviour, a dog — emblem of unholy men — teachers and persecutors — suckling her litter of blind cubs — an echo of Spiritual blindness in which the children of this world are born — the thistle grows beside them. Over our Lord's head a flight of seven doves — the fulness of the Spirit. The Shepherd folding the sheep and lambs — they flocking to him over the green pastures — bulked in the light of the setting sun. The Lake of Galilee beyond — dotted with fishing craft and the crescent moon rising.

A piece of pomogranate peel, a symbol of immortality can be seen and the doves escaping from the city to the light and liberty into which the blind man will emerge.

Above the picture is Rossetti's badge and motto — "Frangas non Flectus" — You shall break, you shall not bend. At the bottom of the picture is "The Light Shineth in darkness". Across both lights are the words, "To the glory of God and in memory of my dear son Gabriel Chas Dante Rossetti Born in London May 12 1828 Died at Birchington Easter Day 1882."

In 1902, the Parish Church was broken into by two thieves who obtained entrance by breaking the lower light of the window. The two thieves were captured and the window repaired by Mr. Shields and William Rossetti.

Shortly after Rossetti died, the bungalow — then named "Cliffside" was sold, it was bought by Mr. F. Osbourne O'Hagen, a millionaire, who changed the name to "Rossetti". He made some alterations but the actual bungalow remained very much the same. He furnished the drawing room which was Rossetti's studio, with beautiful carpets, tapestries, valuable paintings, bronzes and priceless works of art. After Mr. O'Hagen's death in 1930 his daughter, Miss Agnes Greenwood O'Hagen lived in the bungalow until her death in 1952.

In August 1952 the bungalow and site of approximately ¾ acre, were sold by public auction for £4,500, to be followed soon after by the sale of the furniture and effects.

A few years later the bungalow was pulled down and in 1966 the site was "developed" by the building of town houses.

During the First World War the bungalow was used as a Red Cross Hospital for wounded Servicemen, and an air raid shelter 65 feet deep was constructed under the length of the grounds from Rossetti Road to Beach Avenue. This shelter was used on occasions during the Second World War. During the occupation of Manston aerodrome by the United

States Air Force during the Second World War the bungalow was occupied by the American Commanding Officer.

In 1979 a plaque was fixed to a house in Shakespeare Road stating that Rossetti once lived near.

SMUGGLERS AND COASTGUARDS IN BIRCHINGTON

Smuggling has taken place along the coast from Reculver to the east of Birchington for some hundreds of years and there are a number of stories of encounters with smugglers along this stretch of coast. There are still a few houses in Birchington which have cellars or reputed bricked up tunnels which are said to have been used by smugglers for the hiding and storing of their goods.

Two hundred years ago, smuggling was regarded as an honourable occupation for some men of this coast when Birchington's lonely shore was the scene of some stirring fights between bands of smugglers and the representatives of the law.

Since very early times the evasion of customs duties has been a feature of life along our coasts specially along the Kent coasts. The evasion of payment of duty on certain imported goods was practised whenever possible by smuggling goods such as tobacco, spirits specially Geneva Gin, silk goods and tea. The Kent coast being such a short distance from the French and Flemish coasts, smuggling attempts were prevalent in the area and the authorities concentrated more on these south eastern coasts than elsewhere round England's shores to prevent this happening.

The wars of the 18th century led to the imposition of very high duties on tea, spirits, silks and tobacco which resulted in a great increase in "Free Trade", the expression used often for smuggling. The coast line from Reculver to Birchington was specially a most convenient and easy landing beach.

In the 18th century, officers called Riding Officers were appointed to patrol these parts of the coast used by the smugglers. In 1771, a Riding Officer lived in Laburnum House, Station Road, who insured his house and stable with the Sun Alliance Insurance Company as the Sun Insurance Fire Mark on the building shows. His duty was to patrol on horse back, the stretch of coast of Birchington and the pathways leading from the coast and he had the authority to stop and search suspicious carts, pack horses etc., for smuggled goods.

In the Parish Churchyard is a memorial stone against the east wall of the south porch of the Church in memory of a Thomas Thunder, who was upward of 40 years Riding Officer of this parish and who died aged 79 years in 1789.

In 1818, shore bases of the Coast Blockade were set up to combat and suppress the gigantic system of "Free Trade". The trade had grown unchecked during the long wars with France and the Revenue was annually defrauded of many millions of pounds. A station was opened up about every three miles along the coast, each in charge of an officer, a midshipman and about 8 seamen. Birchington came in the Centre Division of the Coast Blockade. There was a station at St. Nicholas, quite near Plumb Pudding Island at the Point, and at Epple on the sea side of Epple Bay Avenue, on top of the cliff overlooking Epple Bay. There was another station at Westgate and at Margate. These Birchington Stations are marked on the Birchington Tithe Map of 1840. The slipway to the sea from the station at Epple can still be seen.

When the National School in Park Lane was opened in 1848, the children from the St. Nicholas Station walked from the Station to the school every day except when the weather was very inclement and in winter time. The following is an entry in the School Log Book for November 9th, 1863,

> Elizabeth Edward, Freeman Everall, Henry and Willam England and Adelaide Ellen and William Corney who all live at the St. Nicholas Station of the Coastguard left for the winter the way being dangerous — indeed William Corney who came to bring me notice was blown over the cliff on his way here. Fortunately he was but little hurt.

In 1831, the Blockade became the Preventive Water Guard and in 1846 it became the Coast Guard.

It seems as if quite a number of Birchington people were involved in this smuggling traffic as is shown by the following entry in the Vestry Book, volume 1 for December 1804 when it was agreed, "that any person who have gristing (corn for grinding) of ye parish who neglects a days work on wrecking or smuggling without the leave of ye Master they work for shall have no gristing that week." At that time food was dear, wages low and many men unemployed, so the Overseers of the Poor let "ye people who have no steady master have gristing — that is one gallon per head per week." So it is quite understandable that some of the energetic men resorted to smuggling and wrecking whenever possible.

In 1746, it was reported to the Commissioners of Revenue that a gang of about 150 smugglers landed their cargo between Reculver and Birchington and went from the sea coast westwards. It was reported there were 63 men and 80 or 90 horses and some went from the landing place to Whitstable and Faversham, and some over Grove Ferry.

The Kentish Gazette supplies some information on smuggling in this area.

> 1805 Dec. 26 Friday and Saturday were seized by the revenue officers at Birchington 250 half-ankers of brandy and Geneva which were conveyed to H.M.

> storehouse at Canterbury.
> 1806 May 22 119 half-ankers of contraband spirits seized between St. Nicholas and Birchington.

On the night of July 22nd, 1820, there was reported another "forced run" near Birchington Minnis when a horse and cart with its load of tubs were seized together with 5 smugglers who the following morning were taken before a Justice of the Peace for Margate and committed to Dover jail. On this occasion there was a singular display of sympathy with the smugglers which took place outside the Court House where an enormous crowd gathered during the trial in the hope of affecting a rescue.

In November 1777, two Excise Officers and six dragoons courageously attacked 150 smugglers on Birchington sands shooting their horses from under them and capturing eight gallons of brandy, 96 gallons of Geneva and 126 pounds of tea.

In the Burial Register of the Parish of Birchington is the following entry,

> 1814 Mar 19th Thomas Hollands, Smuggler, B. 34 years.

There are no other details about him.

In the Churchwardens' Account Book is the following entry,

> 1818 Craved the sess of John Darby 1s, Richard Darby 1s 6d, Elias Darby 1s 6d and James Darby 1s 6d. These four brothers it is supposed were all drowned at sea.

In the Burial Register of the Parish is this entry,

> 1818 Apr 27 John Darby B. 45.

But the newspaper version is somewhat different,

> 1818 April 20th Found dead on the shore between Birchington and Reculver John Darby of Birchington. It is supposed he was engaged in his occupation of smuggling and that being alone he was brutally murdered by some Frenchmen for the sake of his watch and other property which he was known to have had about his person.
>
> An inquest was held and a verdict brought in as above. His three brothers went lately to the French coast and never returned, and are supposed to have drowned in their nefarious trade.
>
> From the Kentish Gazette, April 28th.

A well known Birchington smuggler was John Eastland who was before the magistrate in October 1819. The following entry in the Poor Book throws some light on his occupation.

> 1819 Oct 26. Francis Neame was paid what he gave
> John Eastland when he was before the Magistrate
> and was sent to Dover Jail by ye Preventive Men
> for picking up a Tubb of Liqr on ye Sea Shore 4s 3d.

His wife and family were given money while he was in jail — they had 15s as he had 7 children. A petition was drawn up by Mr. Boys, Attorney, to liberate John Eastland which cost £1 1s 0d.

The last reputed Birchington smuggler was "Jimmy Landy" whose real name was James Eastland. He is supposed to have lived in one of the cottages at Quex, where he was a carpenter, but his hobby was that of smuggling. He is supposed to have smuggled tobacco and spirits to the Shingles at Minnis Bay. The "gobbies" or coast guards used to attempt to catch him by hiding in the sluice at Minnis. He often sold his smuggled goods in the Powell Arms. He was caught on one occasion and sentenced at Sandwich to six months in prison. He died in 1906, in Perfects Cottages aged 82, and was buried in the Parish Churchyard under the name of Huntley. Some of the occupiers of Quex were interested in Landy's smuggling, so it is said.

The present Coastguard Cottages and the Officers' Houses at Minnis Bay and at Epple were built about 1880. At Minnis they were the first houses there, after the Bay Cottage. The coastguards at Minnis did much towards the building of the Congregational Church, now the United Reformed Church. The coastguards ceased to live in the houses at the beginning of the century.

In 1874, there was a boating accident at the Epple Station when two coastguards were drowned and the Vicar and Churchwardens at the time collected over £550 for the benefit of the two widows and the nine children.

In Birchington Churchyard, opposite the Vestry door south of the pathway, are two tombstones to the memory of two Excisemen, and the following inscription probably refers to a tragic occurance,

> At the top is a representation of two hands clasped in
> a sort of grip,
> Officers of Excise

JOHN SMITH	HENRY NEVIL
died the 27th	died the 29th
of Octr 1746	of April 1745
Aged 25	Aged 59
years	years

> Two Gagers here have met a fatal doom
> One past his Prime ye other in his bloom
> Whose Truth and Justice bore an equal Scale
> And Christian Virtues did o'er vice prevail.

Only the burial of John Smith is recorded in the Burial Register.

The Rev. R. H. Barham in "The Ingoldsby Legends" has a poem "The Smugglers Leap, A Legend of Thanet", and describes how a Riding Officer, called Anthony Gill pursued a smuggler, Smuggler Bill, from Reculver to the top of Minster Hill, and both lost their lives in a fog by going over the edge of a chalk pit, now known as Smugglers Leap, near the Prospect Inn. It is said that the smugglers horse only was found crushed beneath its rider. This spot, so it is said, has been haunted ever since. According to the Kentish Gazette of 1769, there was an Exciseman named Gill stationed at Folkestone.

The Canterbury Journal of January 29th 1771, has an account of how Officers of Excise and a soldier found in a chalk pit at Sarre, half-ankers of brandy and gin, and tea which they seized but were attacked by a large gang of 30 smugglers armed with whips loaded at the ends with lead. The Officers resisted and charged the smugglers with sword in hand and fought them but the smugglers got away with most of the smuggled goods. Two of the gang were taken captive and lodged in Canterbury gaol.

Smuggling still goes on to-day.

THE BOUNDS OF THE PARISH AND THE BEATING OF THE BOUNDS

The custom of beating the bounds of the parish is one of the oldest customs known, but unfortunately in recent years the custom has ceased, but perhaps when Birchington again has a Parish Council, the custom will be revived. Parochial perambulations or processions were customary from early times on the three days before Holy Thursday, or Ascension when Litanies were sung for the prevention of pestilence or plague, and for a blessing on the fields and crops. Hence the days were usually called Rogation Days. This was the traditional manner of securing the maintenance of the ancient bounds of the parish, the Rogation tide perambulation or the beating of the bounds. The custom is referred to in the injunction of Queen Elizabeth I who ordained that at convenient places the Curate should admonish the people to give thanks to God, and Psalms 103 and 104 were to be recited.

> Psalm 103 is "Praise the Lord, O my soul, and all that is within me praise His Holy Name."
>
> Psalm 104 is "Praise the Lord, O my soul, O Lord my God, thou art become exceeding glorious."

And the Minister should say such sentences as,

> "cursed is he that transgresseth the bounds or doles of his neighbour."

With the view of perpetuating the knowledge of the exact limitations of the parish a number of boys, usually choirboys, were always taken armed with white willow wands with which to smite the various boundary marks, and that their memories might be impressed they themselves came in for a share of the beating.

Birchington boundaries were marked by stones except in about two places, and there were the special objects the boys had to hit. Beating the bounds was always a festive occasion as the entries in the Churchwardens' Account show.

The old boundaries of Birchington start on the west from the coast near Plum Pudding Island, then follows the Brook stream to include Great Brook End Farm to Little Brook End Farm. Here it passes through the kitchen of the farm house. Here it was customary to put a small boy into the oven in the kitchen and out again, as the bolundary ran through the farm house. Part of the house is in Birchington and part in the Parish of St. Nicholas. From here the boundary passes along the Crispe Road to include St. Nicholas Court Farm and then goes across the fields to Acol Hill Farm. The Boundary between Acol and Birchington then passed along the Acol Birchington Road towards Birchington for about 132 yards and then across direct to Quex. The Acol Parish cut out a long rectangular piece of land from the Park, and the boundary passed through the Quex Mansion on the west side — it is stated through the front door. Here it was customary to put a small boy through a window of Quex Mansion. Because the boundary passed through the Mansion there were several disputes as to which parish was responsible if any of the servants living at Quex had to be relieved by the Overseers of the Poor. It seems as if the Crispes looked after their own poor, but in the time of Mrs. Wiat, who was Frances Crispe and sister of Anna Gertruy Crispe, the time of George I, the Park and the mansion were let to various persons, and at one time the house was let to two different families. Some persons then became chargeable to the parish and the question was hotly fought at meetings, and counsel's opinion was taken whether Acol was their parish or Birchington. The case caused great commotion and no little expense. Eventually it was agreed in 1736 that whatsoever charge may arise for the maintenance of the poor from the house called 'Queax now in the occupation of Francis Neam, that the parishioners of both parishes, that is Birchington and the Vill of Acol, shall jointly contribute to the payment of such charges.''

The boundary then went back to the Shottendane Road to Sparrow Castle Farm, where part of the buildings were in Acol and part in Birchington. Now the boundary zig-zags across the Park to Somali Farm in Park Road. From here it passes across the fields, once marked by numerous stones, to the east of King Ethelbert School. The boundary crosses the Canterbury-Margate Road in a straight line to the sea, crossing the railway line to the east of Ray House. There is still a boundary stone on Cliff Road east of Ray House, with a capital B on one side and a capital W on the other. Ray house was demolished in 1989.

The earliest reference to Beating the Bounds dates from 1531 in the Churchwardens' Account Book.

    1531 Itm to the p'cession of
                Wodchurche in brayd &
                Drynke   VId
                Itm for beryng of the
                cross in the goyng day
                to Wylliam Stoylle   iiiid

William Stoylle occupied one of the Church shops for which he paid a yearly rent of iis. 4d was a day's pay then.

1537	Itm to the pcessyon in the Rogacion weyke in brayd and drynke	Viid
1622	Itm for or dinners when we went ye bounds of ye pishe	0 8s 2d

After the restoration of 1660, there appears to be extravagance at the expense of ratepayers.

1663	Itm expended when wee went the bounds of the pishe for bread, beire, fish, tobacco, meate, and butter for the pishioners	01 10s 0d
1665	May At our Parish bounds May 14th They paid to John Manly & Robt Cotton for bread, beere, meate & dressing	2 13s 6d
1680	June 7 pd at the Rombellashon	0 14s 8d
1685	May ye 13 paid Henrie Spracklinge for bread, and beere in the That we went the bounds of the parish	0 5s 0d

Henry Sprackling was the Landlord of the Inn in the Square.

The expenses reached their height in 1713 when they came to 04 05s 03d, for meat, bread and beer "when we went the bounds of the parish".

In 1828 "For going the Bounds of the Parish 15s" was given to Daniel Oliphant for meat for dinner at the Powell Arms, and to Geo. Duffell, Landlord of the Powell Arms £1 8s 9½d. And Gilbert Stringer was given 5s for placing the Mark Stones between Birchington and Vill of Wood.

There are a very large number of references to Beating the Bounds in the records. South of the boundary was the parish of Acol, and on the east the parish of Minster used to come down to the sea in a narrow strip by Westgate West Bay.

In 1935, the boundaries were altered when Margate incorporated Birchington, the whole of Quex was taken into the Boro' of Margate, and the Parish of Acol was much reduced in size. When Thanet became a District all the boundaries disappeared.

THE OLD ROADS AND TRACKWAYS OF BIRCHINGTON

The ancient Vill of Birchington was situated round the meeting point of two roads which formed quite a large triangular open space, which later became known as The Square. The two roads were, one from Minster Abbey, by Cleve and Quex, to Birchington and then down to the sea at Gore-end along what is now known as the Minnis Road. The other was from Margate, by Birchington Hall, to Birchington and then down Church Hill to St. Nicholas and on to Sarre, where the ferry over the Wantsum had to be crossed, before proceeding on to Canterbury. Coaches from Margate did not use this road but the "Summer Road" as it was called, along the Shottendane Lane and through Acol.

In the past, roads were not well defined and artificially surfaced as they are to-day. The word high-way implied no more than a right-of-way and might have taken the form of a footpath, bridle way, or a cart way. Until comparatively recent times, until the 1700's, our roads were little more than beaten tracks. If any part of the normal right-of-way became impassable, as it often did, it was legally permissible to travel over adjoining land.

By the Act of 1555, the time of Queen Elizabeth I, the inhabitants of each parish were made responsible for the upkeep of the parts of the roads which lay within the parish. By this Act, Surveyors of the Highways, sometimes known as Waywardens, were to be appointed, who were unpaid and whose job was to supervize the work on the highways. This Act said that those occupying land in the parish were to produce carts with two men to each cart for work on the highways on six appointed days. Other householders had to give his own labour or send a substitute. In 1662, parishioners were allowed to make a Highway Rate and labourers could be hired with this money.

When Birchington first levied a Highway Rate is not known. Highway accounts are rare, probably because they never existed or because some have been lost or destroyed.

In the Birchington Churchwardens' Accounts the names of those appointed as Surveyors of the Highways are recorded. The list is not complete except from 1609 to 1694. From 1695 to 1805 there is no record, but from 1805 to 1844 the names are recorded, when there is a Surveyors' Account Book.

From 1609 to 1631, two Surveyors were appointed, two for Birchington and two for the Vill of Wood. The two Surveyors appointed for Birchington were Henry Pennye and William Jorden. They were appointed at the Vestry Meeting when the Churchwardens and the

THE SQUARE
Birchington, 1870

THE SQUARE
Birchington, early 1900's

STATION ROAD
Birchington, late 1890's

Overseers of the Poor were appointed. In 1631, the first two Surveyors of the Highways for the Vill of Wood were Edward Coleman and Jeffrey Reade. All the leading occupiers and tenants of land took their turn in being Surveyors and occasionally they held the office for two years.

The first mention of work on the highways in Birchington is in 1623 when the following entry occurs in the Churchwardens' Account Book,

    For beere for ye Labourers in
    ye highways   0 1s 6d

and in   1632 Itm for beere for ye
    Labourers in ye highways   0 01s 03d

Most of the work consisted of gathering stones from the fields in baskets or from the sea shore and filling up the holes in the roads. The Birchington Surveyors' Account Book, which opens in 1805, gives much information on road repairing and how it was paid for. The book opens with an Assessment and a list of tenants and occupiers of land who were assessed for the rapair of the highways at sixpence in the pound rent. The highest assessed was John Friend for Brooksend. He had to pay £7 16s 8d. Next came Benjamin Bushell for the Parsonage who was assessed at £7 12s 6d. There were 50 ratepayers, 33 paid less than 10s. The total collected was £47 18s 3d.

Some were rated for a "Team" at £1 7s 0d and had to send a wagon or two carts for 6 days, a team being equal to £50 rent. A half a team was a cart with one horse for 6 days. These had to be supplied after proper notice given by the Surveyors, but it was really a voluntary scheme. It appears that those assessed for repairing the highways could either supply horses and carts or pay the rate. A number of small ratepayers had no horses or carts so had to pay in cash.

Stones were collected from the fields and were paid for at the rate of 1s per cart load of 20 baskets. Beach stones from the sea shore was paid for at the same rate. The Surveyors in 1805 were John Friend and James Neame.

Unemployed men and men from the Workhouse were employed in the work of filling in the holes in the roads.

In 1807, Gilbert Stringer, Treasurer of the Birchington Workhouse was paid £27 18s 11d for the use of men from the Workhouse who collected stones from the fields and spread them over the roads. In 1810, men were paid 2s per day for this work and families, women and children were paid 1s per load for picking up stones. From the Surveyors' Book,

    1810/11 May 3rd paid Knotts
    family picking 5 load of
    stones   5s 0d

Paid Philpotts wife for picking 12½ loads of stones	12s 6d
Paid Knotts wife and family picking 32 load of stones on Mr. George Friends Sheep walk	£1 12s 0d

The Surveyors supplied the baskets which cost 10p each.

It seems as if at this time Gilbert Stringer supervised the men working on the roads.

The roads at this time, that is at the beginning of the 19th century, were in a very bad state as carriages from Monkton and Minster were forbidden to carry beach through the parish in wet weather and notices were issued about this. Most of the roads had large pot holes and ruts and there was no drainage. In order to help the drainage of the roads, men were employed in digging out the sides of the roads and paid 2½d per rod (5½ yards). This was done in March when the road at the end of "ye Street towards Margate" was dug out.

The road from Canterbury by the Pond and through the Square to Margate was known as the Street. It was much narrower than now. The road went by the Mill which, up to 1772, was close to the road so that the sweeps as they turned round frightened horses. As a result the Mill was moved back 60 years as reported in the Kentish Gazette of that year. The removal was done in little more than a day with the utmost ease and by the assistance of two horses, although it is stated that the weight was upwards of 40 tons and neither the sweeps nor the mill stones were removed.

The road passed by the Pond, at the bottom of Church Hill, on the south side. This pond was filled in in 1933 and now, after very heavy rain, this spot is often flooded. The farm on the site of the present Church House was known as Street Farm. The word Street is on the 1688 map of Birchington stolen from the Parish Church in 1958.

The other highway or really, trackway, was a narrow lane coming from Minster going by Cleve and Quekes, through the Square and down to the sea at Gore-end. This trackway from Quekes to the Square was known as Parish Lane — it is now known as Park Lane. The late Mr. Charles Gambrill, for many years the verger at the Parish Church said in his "Memories" of 1904 that there were some old cottages at the entrance to Park Lane, and that there was just room "to get a waggon load of corn up that road", showing how narrow it was. This way then ran through the village, by the old Malt House, now the Vegetable Factory, by Upper Gore End Farm to the sea near Lower Gore-end Farm.

BIRCHINGTON FROM THE S.W.
Showing the Pond, Canterbury Road

1898 The Sea Breeze Cycle Factory where the first Ladies' cycle was invented.

It was situated at the junction of the Station Road and the Minnis Road. The site was occupied by Benefield and Cornfords Estate Office. Later a part of the building became a Grocers Shop — Fashams. The Cycle Factory was owned by a Mr. George Cousins, a prominent Birchington man who at one time was the Chairman of the old Parish Council. It was here that the first Lady's cycle was invented and built but it was never patented.

SEABREEZE,
CYCLES
FOR EITHER SEX.
The Popular Exhibit of the Stanley Cycle Shows.

GEO. COUSINS, Patentee & Manufacturer, BIRCHINGTON-ON-SEA, KENT.

The Seabreeze Cycles are built on *Hygienic* lines.
The *Spring Frame* obviates the need of *pneumatic tyres*.
The *Fairy Seabreeze* (rigid frame) *an Ideal Lady's Bicycle*.
The *Diamond Frame*. Preventative of the hideous bicycle hump.

An advertisement for a Lady's Cycle made and invented at the Sea Breeze Cycle Factory by George Cousins at the end of the 1800s.

Another old trackway was the "way to the sea" as marked on the 1688 map of Birchington. It is now known as Albion Road and Colemans Stairs Road. The Coleman family, who once lived in the farm house now known as The Smugglers, farmed land adjoining this road as did the Neames. Some old inhabitants of Birchington remember this road being called Pig Lane and as Wilsons Road. A Richard Wilson owned land along this road in the early 1800's.

Epple, or Epald Road, is another old roadway. Over one hundred years ago farmers using this road were ordered by the Vestry to take 60 loads of stones to waste ground near the road, for the Surveyors to use to repair the road. Originally, this way went straight to the sea by the Coatsguard Houses but in comparatively recent times, the roadway at the sea end has been diverted and the old gap way filled in. Where Ocean Close is now was once a Brick Field.

There is an old pathway across the fields by Kent Gardens, by Bedlem Cottages, destroyed in 1939 during a Civil Defence Exercise, across the field and railway line, to the sea and along the coast to the St. Nicholas Coast Guard Station. This way was often used by the Riding Officers.

Another old way went from Upper Gore-end Farm, along what is now known as Green Road, originally Green Lane, to the sea at a gap way called, on the old maps, Lime Kiln Gap. Here was once a beacon.

Yet another old way went from Lower Gore-end Farm, along what is now known as Grenham Bay Avenue to the sea at Grenham Gap way. Between Lower and Upper Gore-end Farms was a Brickfield.

An old pathway runs from Mill Row across the fields to Brook End Farm, Hale, to St. Nicholas.

The parish was first lit by 21 gas lamps, in 1876, at a cost of £3 9s 8d per lamp.

It is interesting to note that in 1910, the Parish Council agreed that the speed of motor cars passing through the village to be limited to 8 miles per hour. The first motor car in Birchington was brought by Mr. G. Cousins, who had a cycle shop and factory at the junction of Station Road and Minnis Road.

THE OLD BIRCHINGTON INSTITUTE

THE VILLAGE CENTRE OF ONE HUNDRED YEARS AGO

Birchington to-day has a fine village Community Centre but the village had a village centre over one hundred years ago.

In 1879, the Vicar of Birchington — the Rev. J. P. Alcock — who was the first Vicar of Birchington as, until 1871, Birchington was part of the ecclesiastical parish of Monkton — Major Morrison Bell and a few other prominent gentlemen of the place agreed that the village needed a community centre. As a result, the Vicar, Major Bell and a Mr. C. Moore (who was the Peoples' Churchwarden) borrowed the sum of £500 on mortgage from a Mr. R. White, and purchased the property which became known as the Institute — the first community centre in Birchington.

The Institute was situated in the Square behind what is now a Sweetmarket. The sweet shop was the caretaker's house, but later became the Church Verger's house and for many years a Mr. and Mrs. Gambrill, the Church Verger, lived there. Access to the Institute from the Square was by a narrow passage way by the side of the caretaker's house.

The Institute consisted of a hall with a stage and a gallery, an upstairs room and outhouses. It became the centre for public meetings, concerts, lectures, entertainments, social gatherings etc. It had a Reading Room where newspapers and periodicals could be seen and a Library. In time it became licensed for stage plays. Technical classes were held there, and the Knott Lodge of Oddfellows, formed in 1881 and the Good Intent Benefit Society held their meetings there. The old Parish Councils also held their meetings there.

The Institute appeared to have had a struggling existence. The Trustees, the Rev. Alcock, Major Bell and Mr. C. Moore had hoped that the centre would pay its way and in due time, pay off the mortgage. It is interesting to note that the caretaker paid two shillings a week rent for his cottage. Early in the 1900's' the Trustees offered the property to the Parish Council but there were obstacles in the way preventing the Parish Council taking over the property.

In 1907, the Rev. Serres, the Vicar and Mr. Honeyball, Churchwarden, were appointed Trustees by the Charity Commissioners.

In the 1890's, the first Birchington Infants' School was held in the Institute — before the Primitive Methodist Chapel in Albion Road was used as such. A wood carving class was held here and some of the oak wood carving in the Parish Church was done by this class. In the early 1900's, the girls and boys from the National School in Park Lane had cookery and woodwork classes there. It became the meeting place of the

Birchington Cricket Club and of the village band. During the Second World War it was used by the W.R.V.S. for meals.

In the 1920's there was much correspondence between the then Trustees and the Parish Council regarding the Institute and eventually, early in the 1950's, the Charity Commissioners sold the property, paid off the remaining mortgage, invested the balance and established a scheme to regulate what became known as the Birchington Institute Charity or Fund. The Scheme was sealed by the Commissioners on April 25th 1952. The first Trustees appointed were Frederick Wm. Mellamby, J.P., William R. Curtis of Station Road, Kathleen E. Phillips of Shakespeare Road, Hannah B. Powell Cotton of Quex and Denys H. E. Jeston of Grenham House. The Trustees are appointed from time to time by the Thanet District Council. The income of the Charity is used for any charitable purposes for the benefit of the inhabitants of Birchington not provided out of rates, taxes or other public funds.

Such is something of the first Community Centre in Birchington.

THE STORY OF BIRCHINGTON'S DOG ACRE

WHEN DOGS WENT TO CHURCH — AND WERE 'WHIPPED OUT'

Dog Acre has been much in Birchington news and all Birchingtonians are delighted that this valuable piece of land situated near the centre of the village is now preserved as an open space to be enjoyed by all. It has a long and interesting history.

Originally, with other land in Birchington, it belonged to the Church. "Dog Acre" was a strip of land along the south side of Alpha Road with a small frontage to Station Road. It was near "Butt Acre" where the men of the village practised shooting, usually on Sunday afternoons after attending Church. It is not certain where Butt Acre was but it was probably between "Dog Acre" and the village. In early days the village was situated round the Square and only a little way down what is now called Station Road. The "Buttys" are mentioned in the Church Land Terrier of Henry VIII's reign, 1527, and also in the Terrier made in the reign of Charles I, 1627.

This land was called "Dog Acre" because the village official known as the "Dog Whipper" had this approximately one acre of Church Land for his use, for which he paid no rent — it was one of his "perks".

In days long prior to a dog tax, dogs abounded in great numbers — even more so than now — and almost every cottager possessed one, mainly to aid in fetching the cow or sheep from the common land. These dogs were often in the habit of attending Church with their masters and sat under their masters' seats.

To regulate the behaviour of the dogs and to remove the unseemly from the Church or Churchyard, most parishes possessed a modestly paid official known as the "Dog Whipper". It was his job to remove the offenders, usually by means of wooden tongs which he used for gripping the offending dogs by the neck and carrying them out of the Church.

Later on in Birchington, it became the Dog Whipper's job not only to keep order among the dogs but also to keep order among the boys in the Church, in the Churchyard and sitting on the Church wall.

The earliest reference to Dog Acre and to the Dog Whipper is in the Birchington Churchwardens' Account Book for the year 1622 — the reign of James I, when "Old Hayward" was the dog whipper and received eight shillings per year for this duty and was allowed the acre of Church land free.

In 1623 we read,

> To old Hayward for whipping ye
> dogges out of ye Church one
> whole yeare   8s

Old Hayward was followed by "old Posier" who was paid the same rate. Many such entries appear in the Accounts year after year. In 1687, we read,

> John Taylor dog whipper for his office hath one
> accer of the said (Church) land.

In 1694 we read,

> One accer now lett out Thomas Penny Dog whipper,
> Abutting to the butt accer.

Later on, the Dog Whipper walked round the Church twice every Sunday, during service, to keep good order, and was paid by the Churchwardens 6d each Sunday.

On the Birchington Tithe Map of 1840, Dog Acre is marked as being owned by the Churchwardens of Birchington and in the Schedule attached to the Map, it is numbered 312. It was scheduled as arable and was 3 roods 31 poles in area. At that time there was no Alpha Road and there were no houses further down Station Road than what is now the Central garage, except for three small cottages on the east side of the road about opposite the multiple stores.

On the 1st Edition of the large scale Ordnance Survey Map, scale 25 inches to the mile, published in 1872, for Birchington, this piece of land is marked "DOG ACRE", No. 54 and it is named in the book of reference to the map. At that time there was still no Alpha Road.

In 1921, Dog Acre was sold by the Church authorities for £390 6s 9d and the money invested by the Charity Commissioners in 5% War Stock, the small income from which is used to try to keep the Churchyard clean and in good order.

Later it was acquired by the Ministry of Public Buildings and Works on behalf of the Post Office Corporation who at one time intended to build on it a Post Office and Sorting Office but that plan was abandoned.

The present piece of land is not quite the same size and shape as it was originally when the Church first had it several hundreds of years ago.

Most Birchington residents are grateful to all those who were instrumental in persuading the Thanet District Council to preserve Dog Acre as an open space and to convert it into a public park, even though so small.

THE STORY OF THE FOUNTAIN IN THE SQUARE

It was in October 1896 that at a meeting of rate payers, that it was decided that a lamp in the centre of the Square, to commemorate Queen Victoria's Jubilee, would be fitting and desirable. Some two months later, when the same rate payers met to discuss the matter further, a resolution in favour of a drinking fountain in the Square was carried but when the matter of raising the money to pay for it was broached, little support was forthcoming and so the matter was dropped.

At a meeting of the Parish Council in 1900, the Chairman announced that the brother of Major Morrison Bell suggested that as a memorial to Major Bell, he would erect a drinking fountain, with a trough for horses and dogs, and surmounted by a lamp. Major Morrison Bell had been a great benefactor to the village and the Chairman stated that he was sure that all would agree that this would be a fitting memorial to him. So it was decided to write to Mr. Bell, thanking him for his offer and stating that the parishioners would be asked to express their opinions on the suggestion. This was done and so 511 parishioners were issued with voting cards to vote on the idea, which resulted in 330 voting in favour, with only 15 against and 166 cards were not returned. Such was the result of Birchington's first "card vote".

At the next meeting of the Council, after the result of the card vote was known, a long and animated and at times acrimonious discussion took place. Two Councillors, Messrs. Pointer and Pemble were totally hostile to the idea. Mr. Pointer stated that there never had been any erection in the middle of the Square in his time, or in his father's time and he did not intend that there should be one in anybody else's time if he could prevent it. He declared that if the fountain was erected, they would always have to have a policeman there to regulate the traffic and it would no longer be possible for waggonettes to drive up and turn safely in the middle. He also stated that it would be dangerous to cross the Square so that mothers would almost be frightened to send thir children to school if they had to cross the Square. This last remark caused much laughter. Mr. Pemble supported him stating that he did not want anything in the Square. In spite of this opposition, a resolution was passed "having ascertained by a poll of the parish that a large majority of the parishioners are in favour of accepting the offer of Mr. Bell, the Clerk be instructed to write to Mr. Bell accepting the same, subject to the approval of the design."

In due time the design was submitted to the Parish Council and a resolution was passed thanking Mr. Bell for the very handsome fountain

REV. H. A. SERRES, VICAR OF BIRCHINGTON
Conducting the Service

he proposed to erect in the Square and that the County Council and the Rural District Council (Eastry Rural District Council) be asked for their sanction. Messrs, Pointer and Pemble voted against the resolution — the only two.

On October 20th, the Surveyor to the Kent County Council met the members of the Parish Council in the Square for a "site" meeting, but it was a long time before the Parish Council received the reply. At the November meeting of the Parish Council, a letter from the District Council was received stating that they considered a fountain at the place suggested would be a danger to vehicular traffic and that they had informed the County Council accordingly.

The County Council did not reply until the following February when a letter was received by the Parish Council stating that the "the Roads Committee have decided to recommend the Council not to oppose such erection provided your Council will let me have their undertaking that the fountain shall be kept well lighted at night as otherwise there will be danger to road traffic. Your Council will understand that the County Council has no power to sanction the obstruction but merely decided to take no action to prevent it. This will not prevent any member of the public, who may be aggrieved from taking steps for its removal." Councillors Pointer and Pemble were delighted with the outcome so far.

A copy of the letter was sent to Mr. Bell and his reply was read out at the March meeting of the Parish Council. His reply was, "As it appears from this letter (the County Council letter) that if this fountain was put up, it is in the power of a cantankerous person to take steps to have it removed, I feel that I have no option but to recall my offer as I do not wish to be the immediate cause of a village wrangle. I regret the trouble I have caused your Council in suggesting this matter which I had hoped might have considered to be a public use, but as red taperism, probably suggested by some local dissentient, has decided otherwise I shall give the money that this fountain would have cost to the Margate Sea Bathing Infirmary, which my brother always took a great interest in, provided of course, they will accept it."

This development was quite unexpected and several letters appeared in the "Isle of Thanet Gazette" expressing regret at the loss of the fountain and that base ingratitude had been shown to Mr. Bell. The withdrawal came just six days before the Annual Parish Meeting when the election of the Parish Councillors took place for the ensuing years and Messrs. Pointer and Pemble were for re-election. It is certain they wondered what would happen at the election as indignation at the loss of the fountain was then at fever pitch and there was no doubt that they were responsible for the withdrawal of the offer.

There was considerable excitement at the Annual Meeting when there were 11 candidates for the 9 seats, and attempts were made to put questions concerning the drinking fountain but the Chairman would not allow them stating that the fountain was now lost, so need not be referred to again. Messrs. Pointer and Pemble were asked questions but they both evaded the issue. Pointer did state that if elected, he would resign in favour of his son and that he would have nothing more to do with the Council. In fact Pointer was elected — he came 5th — but he did not resign.

The village now had to wait until 1909 before it got the present fountain. It was the gift of Alderman Grant in memory of his wife. The inscription on the fountain reads, "Gratefully accepted by the inhabitants of Birchington from Alderman Grant." Alderman Grant lived at Fernleigh, Canterbury Road, which later became a Boys' Preparatory School called Birchington House and then was incorporated into Queen Bertha's Girls School, and this school in time was demolished to become part of the Queen Bertha's Housing Estate.

The fountain was opened on 2nd June 1909, when the Rev. H. A. Serres, the Vicar of Birchington at the time, conducted the service. A large number of Birchington people attended the opening including the children from the National School in Park Lane.

It has been moved on a few occasions. When it was first erected, it was in the centre of the Square, then it moved nearer to the Church Gates and in recent years, near to the shops on the south side of the Square. Prior to the First World War, when there was little traffic, stalls were set up in the Square against the fountain, especially on a Saturday.

THE RAILWAYS OF BIRCHINGTON

THE RAILWAY THAT ONCE RAN FROM MINNIS BAY TO MANSTON

The coming of the railway to Birchington in October 1863, gave a considerable impetus to the growth and development of the place. At first the railway was just an extension of the line from Faversham through to Ramsgate, of the London, Chatham and Dover Railway and ranked only as a second main line.

The Margate Railway Act of 1859 authorised the first extension of the line from Faversham and the Kent Coast Railway Act of 1861, took the line through to Ramsgate. The line from Chatham to Faversham was at first a single line. The first main line was from Faversham through to Canterbury and on to Dover.

The line reached Herne Bay from Faversham in 1857. East of Herne Bay the line had to cross comparatively high ground and the railway gradient on Blacksole Bank was 1 in 93. Beyond the summit the railway ran down to the Wantsum into Thanet. Here was four miles of almost straight and level track — in fact over 2½ miles was absolutely straight and level but it was this section that was inundated by the floods of 1953 which necessitated the building of the earthworks running parallel to the railway line to protect it in the future.

The 8 mile gap between Herne Bay and Birchington was too lengthy for the traditional block signalling so roughly at the midway point, in an isolated marsh land setting, was placed the Reculvers signal box. This box was done away with some years ago.

The line from Herne Bay to Margate through Birchington was opened 3rd September 1863 but public service did not begin until 2nd October 1863.

The Birchington Station was built at the same time as the line and in 1878, was named Birchington-on-Sea. By this time the north of the railway line was being developed and becoming a seaside resort. The station buildings including the distinctive station house with prominent gables were placed on the "up" side facing the inland village. The Station House was probably designed by J. P. Seddon and John Taylor who designed and built the bungalows and other houses on the north side of the railway. There were originally two signal boxes, the "A" box on the "up" side and the "B" box on the "down" side. Both are no longer in existence.

Each week the Kebles Gazette published the Time tables of the London, Chatham and Dover Railway. The fare in 1867 from Margate to Birchington was 3d — third class and from Margate to London, third class, 6s 2d, cheap fast train.

140

At first, before the present brick bridge over the railway, there was a crossing and then a wooden bridge but these were soon replaced by the brick bridge.

With the opening of the railway in October 1863, it was possible to go by train from Birchington to London, to Ludgate Hill or Victoria, easily and comfortably. Birchington now began to develop as a healthy seaside resort within reasonable train distance from London. From now on the population of the place began to grow quite considerably.

Few people of the present generation know that once there was a single track railway line which ran from Minnis Bay, across the fields to Manston Airfield. It was constructed early in 1916, during the First World War, for the purpose of carrying supplies, goods and aeroplane parts to the airfield by rail. The airfield was then a Royal Naval Air Service Station which had been transferred from St. Mildred's Bay, Westgate.

The line was nearly 3 miles long, laid on cinders and of a new American pattern, now known as flat-bottomed, and instead of being bolted to the sleepers was "dogged" or clipped.

The line joined the main North Kent Line on the "up" side near the site of the old Birchington "A" signal box which was demolished in 1929, and very near where the footpath over the fields from Essex Gardens crosses the main line at Horsa Road. From here the track went across the fields to the Canterbury Road which it crossed about 80 yards west of King Edward Road. It then continued across the fields to the Acol Road, which it crossed just below the short fir-tree lined private road leading to Quex Park. It then proceeded over the field crossing the B 2049 road and then on to near Sparrow Castle Water Pumping Station. From here it ran parallel to the Manston Road, crossing the road leading to Cheeseman's Farm, to the airfield at near Pounces. It terminated near Pounces where there was a long platform and a siding alongside a hanger and workshops. Where the line crossed the roads there were gates across the track, which were opened by the guard.

At the Minnis Bay end there was a long siding into which the carriages were shunted from the main line until ready to be taken to Manston. Usually a small tank engine was used on this line but occasionally, main line steam engines were used. The line had no signals and all the points were hand worked.

On occasions, Service Personnel were issued railway tickets at Manston and travelled by the train from Manston to Birchington where the coaches were attached to the main line trains.

The line was taken up and demolished in about 1928. Its route can still be seen in places where it crosses the fields — the corn does not grow quite so well on the track. At Manston, rails could have been seen in the coal yard, as well as the old unloading platform but it is now a private housing estate.

Local boys from Acol, going to school in Park Lane at this time, used to put pennies on the line where it crossed the Acol Road for the train to run over them and they were known to jump on to the train for a short ride until chased off.

The track of this railway is marked on the One Inch Ordnance Map Sheet 117 dated 1920 but not on large scale maps.

All that remained of the RAILWAY that once ran from MINNIS BAY to MANSTON Showing the railway lines in the old coalyard which was once the terminus

SOME INTERESTING HOUSES IN BIRCHINGTON

Up to the middle of the 19th century Birchington village was situated mainly round what is now known as the Square, where several of its ancient houses remain in spite of demolitions and the re-erection of modern premises. There are at least four of the Charles II and of the William III Flemish period buildings, with their characteristic Dutch stepped gables and old fashioned fitments. They are Grove House, Laburnum House, The Smugglers and The Pewter Pot. These have been scheduled under the Registration of Ancient Monuments Act and with others, are listed by the Department of the Environment as buildings of special architectural and historic interest. The older generation of villagers used to designate them as the "Dykers" houses, probably because they associated them with the Hollanders who were introduced into this area at this particular time to advise and superintend the building of the sea wall defences and the draining of the marshes to the west of Thanet. These houses were built of brick with prettily curved gable ends. Perhaps there is no part of Kent which retains, within an equally small area, so many examples of these graceful gables as does the Isle of Thanet. Such houses with these gables can be seen in Minster, Reading Street and Broadstairs. There were several other houses round or near the Square that had the characteristic Dutch stepped gables, which have now been demolished or altered so much. Bath Cottages in Station Road, at the junction with Albion Road, before they were demolished had a Flemish gable overlooking Albion Road.

GROVE HOUSE

This house is approached by a tree shaded paved pathway from the Square. The main portion of the building is constructed of dark red brick in what is technically known as the Flemish Bond. It has Dutch gables on both ends. The house may originally have been two houses or cottages. On the two main gable heads are two different sets of initials, on the northern one is I.M., which can just be made out and on the southern gable appear the initials I.C. These initials are at the end of iron tie rods passing through the masonry to engage the main timbers within the building, thereby knitting and strengthening the fabric generally. The house has a cellar with a trapdoor to the hall floor above. It may have been a secret hide-away in the old smuggling days.

The Covell family may have lived in the original house. The Covell family appear much in Birchington history, occupying all the official village positions. A Robert Covell was Deputy in 1614, Overseer of the Poor also in 1614 and later was Churchwarden in 1625. The initials I.C. probably stand for John Covell. The initials I.M. may stand for Isabella Masters, but there is no record of Isabella Masters in the Parish Registers.

On the building are three Fire Marks showing that the house was insured with the Sun Insurance Company who state that in 1757, Fenttin Covell of Birchington, Blacksmith, insured his brick and tiled dwelling house, his household goods, his barn, stable and Smith's forge for £400 and that in 1805, John Covell of Chatham, gentleman, insured the house and the smith's forge in the tenure of Edward Young, Blacksmith, and a house in the tenure of John Sidders, farmer, for £400.

Adjoining Grove House was the Blacksmith's Forge, owned in 1678 by Mary East, who carried out the iron work necessary in the repair of the Parish Church at this time.

From the Churchwardens' Accounts for 1687,

To Mary East Smithes for 92 lb of window bars at 3½d ye pound	1 6 10
To the said Mary for speek (nails) & plate	0 0 10
To ye said Mary for mendinge ye bell guggens (gudgeons)	0 1 6

The smithy is now a garage and a motor repair workshop.

The present house is probably the two cottages joined together sometime between 1650 and 1700.

LABURNUM HOUSE — STATION ROAD

This house is a listed Grade II building of two storeys and an attic, built of brown brick with red brick dressing. The roof has Dutch shaped gables at the ends but unlike Grove House and the Smugglers, has no ownership letters or figures that function as wall anchors. In this house are plain iron bands with foliated ends which pass through the masonry to strengthen the fabric.

On the front of the house is an old Fire Mark with the number 283720 on it. The mark indicates that the brick and tiled house was insured in 1770, with the Sun Alliance Insurance Company, by Richard Laurence Bowles of Birchington, Officer of Customs, for £250, his household goods for £50. Near was a thatched house in the tenure of Michael Hughes, Labourer and insured for £30 and an adjoining brick and tiled house in the tenure of John Birch, was insured for £70. Preventive Officer, Richard Laurence Bowles was married twice in the Parish Church, first to Bridget Winsley of Canterbury in 1754 and then to a widow, Eleanor Merry in 1809.

LABURNUM HOUSE, STATION ROAD 1960

The present house was built in 1765 or 1766 by Daniel and John Jarvis of Deal, or possible their mother who was a widow. It was built on part of a 3 rod plot which was the garden to an older property mentioned in the original deeds of 1619. The original site belonged to Thomas Grenefelde, who was Curate at Birchington, who also bought a plot of land called the Butts. The Tithe Map of 1840, lists the house when it was probably called Mulberry House and the 1st Edition of the 25 inch Ordnance Survey Map of 1872 shows two houses with a tree, maybe a Mulberry tree or a Laburnum tree, in the road outside. This tree was still there within living memory and had a seat built round it on which the locals used to sit.

The older house was divided into two by a previous Daniel and John Jarvis in 1698 and in the deeds, is a detailed record of how this was done. Five separate plots of land belonged to the property at one time and of these the original 3 rod piece was used to build the present house on 1½ acres called the Butts, where the villagers practised shooting, formed part of the property originally.

Thomas Greenfield, the curate of Birchington, was before the Archdeacon's Court in 1619 for unseemly conduct — "hath endeavoured to stir up strife and discontent between Mr. Doctor Clarke, the vicar and the parishioners — and that the said Mr. Greenfield without respect

The East Gable of THE SMUGGLERS
Showing the Flemish gable and the
iron stays with the letters W W

to his function and calling hath demeaned himself very basely in frequenting base company in ale houses — etc." also, "in doing base and servile work as going bare legged to catch fish with ripps (pannier or basket) at his back." In 1622, Thomas Greenfield left Birchington for Goudhurst.

Daniel Friend bought the property from Thomas Greenfield, a member of the well known Birchington family who later became the owners of Birchington Hall.

John Jarvis, who inherited the house in 1722, was a carpenter but later moved to Margate to become a Tidesman. Tidesmen controlled the loading of cargoes and worked very closely with the Preventive men. In 1767, the property was sold to Richard Laurence Bowles, the riding Officer or Preventive Officer.

Later the Neame family acquired the property, who in time, farmed several farms in the area and at one time lived in the Smugglers, then known as Evergreen House.

THE SMUGGLERS

This is a grade II listed house of two storeys and attic, of brown brick with red brick dressings, quoins and stringcourses. The roof has Dutch gables at the ends. This house was formerly known as Evergreen House but was changed to that of The Smugglers in the 1930's when it was opened as a restaurant. Originally it was the farm house and in the early 1800's, a branch of the Neame family lived there.

It was built in the second half of the 1600's. The house has an iron rod passing through the masonry to engage the main timbers within the building and on the end of the rods, on the east gable are the letters W Ⱨ in iron. These initials stand for William Neave, who lived in the house in the 1700's.

In the 1600's, the Coleman family lived there and farmed the surrounding land. Hence the name Colemans Stairs Road and Neame Road.

THE PEWTER POT

Before this inn bore this name it was called the New Inn, but the original New Inn is now the Powell Arms. The building has been extensively altered. It was refronted in the later 19th century. It has Dutch gables. It is marked on the Tithe Map of 1840 as being occupied by a Edward Young. At the end of the last century and the beginning of the present century, there were livery stables in the yard behind and horse brakes started from here in the summer for drives to Minster and Ebbsfleet.

THE POWELL ARMS

This is a Grade II Listed building much altered and renovated. This is probably the oldest inn in Birchington and before 1823, was known as the New Inn. It became the Powell Arms in the September of 1823 in honour of Squire Powell Powell of Quex, who was made High Sheriff of Kent in that year.

It was in this Inn that the Vestry Meetings were held after they had adjourned from the Church and here were held the meetings of the ratepayers when the village officials were appointed, the Churchwardens, the Overseers of the Poor and the Surveyors of the Highways. Here were the Parish Accounts passed and signed and the sesses agreed to.

In the Poor Books, this Inn is referred to by the name of the Landlord, such as Duffells, Blews, Mays.

At the time of the Tithe Map 1840, it was kept by Robert Pinker.

THE QUEEN'S HEAD HOTEL

The interesting feature of this building is the rear elevation which is faced with flints. Tradition states that this was the original Acorn Inn. It is mentioned in the Kentish Gazette of 1768. At the time of the Tithe Map it was kept by Oliver Wanstall.

THE ACORN INN

On the Tithe Map (1840), this Inn is shown as a cottage but in 1802, a Isaac Williams was rated for "the Sign of ye Acorn" and in 1810, George Duffell was rated for the Acorn Public House. It appears from the Poor Books that occasionally travellers with passes, such as soldiers or their wives, stayed for the night at this Inn.

THE SEA VIEW HOTEL

This was built in 1865, soon after the coming of the railway to Birchington and was at first called the Railway Hotel.

COURT MOUNT, CANTERBURY ROAD

The front of this building is late 18th century to early 19th century. The rear wing is timbered framed and has 16th to 17th century beamed ceiling and inglenook fireplace. Like so many of these old buldings, it has been extensively altered. Formerly it was the farmhouse of South End Farm and at the time of the Tithe Map was owned by George Taddy Friend and occupied by John Brooke. He was one of the village officials, that of Surveyor of the Highways in 1836.

Very near was the Pond, on the south side of the Canterbury Road, opposite Sackville. The Pond is marked on the old 1688 map of Birchington and also on the Tithe Map. It was filled in, in 1933 and now, after very heavy rain, this spot is flooded.

OLD COTTAGES
South side of Canterbury Road opposite Churchyard

Originally, these were one house and part of Church Hill Farm. This farm was owned, in 1688, by John Bridges of Canterbury, gentleman, who owned several farms in Thanet. On one house is a Sun Alliance Fire Mark with number 537003. This shows, so the Sun Alliance Insurance Co. say, that the two cottages were insured in 1787 by a Wm. Grigg, of Birchington, a Miller and one house in the tenure of Widow Ayles, for not exceeding £50 each.

OLD COTTAGE
No. 218 Canterbury Road, north side

This is a timber framed cottage extensively altered, partly flint faced and part brick. It has a tiled roof. This was part of Street Farm, which was adjoining the present Church House and included part of the present Churchyard. At the time of the Tithe Map it was owned by John "Birchington" Friend, Esq., of Birchington Hall and occupied by John Brooke.

OLD BAY COTTAGE

This was the farm house of Gore End Farm and as far back as 1310, the land was the property of the great landed proprietor, Sir William Leybourne, who lived at Leybourne Castle, near Maidstone. It is a Grade II listed building. Part of the house is a 15th century timber framed cottage with a tiled roof. The left side of the building is of two storeys, faced with 18th century red brick and with a thatched roof. It has a Sun Alliance Insurance Fire Mark.

CARMEL COURT, SPENCER ROAD

The original Carmel Court was demolished in 1964 to make room for the high rise flats. The original house is said to have been a replica of a villa on or near Mount Carmel in Palestine. In the front, facing Spencer Road, was a fountain. Inside was a bath built like a Roman Bath, with steps leading down to it.

A number of interesting old houses have been demolished in comparatively recent years. Among these are:—

BIRCHINGTON HALL, CANTERBURY ROAD

This was demolished in 1967. At the time of the Tithe Map, this large house was occupied by John "Birchington" Friend, Esq. In very early times there was a house here called Skottestone, for in the year 1278, an inquiry was made by jurymen of Bicheltone, Wode and Monketonne concerning the cutting down of trees and injury to the land at Skottestone by Thomas Esther and Stephen de Atynbroke. The position of Skottestone is difficult to define but there is every probability that Birchington Hall, later to become Spurgeons Seaside Homes, was the site. It was in the 18th century that the large farm house was occupied by several of the Friend family. The large field at the back is still known as Scots Down.

Birchington Hall was a large house consisting of an Outer Hall, Main Hall, four Reception Rooms, twelve Bedrooms and Dressing rooms, Bathroom and domestic offices. The Dining Room had a beamed ceiling with doors opening to a large conservatory. There were two lodges, one for the gardener and the other for the coachman. There were extensive gardens and grounds.

John "Birchington" Friend was an important man in the place and in time held all the Parish Offices. He was also Deputy. Sometimes the house is known as Birchington Hall and sometimes as Birchington Place.

In the 1870's, it was occupied by Thomas Gray and his wife. The grays were very generous to the village and specially to the Parish Church. They gave towards the building of St. Mildred's Church at Acol in 1876 and in 1887 gave generously to the repairing of the Church Spire when the Clock was installed to commemorate Queen Victoria's Jubilee. Mrs. Gray also gave the first Gas fittings in the Church and four stained glass windows in the nave of the Church in memory of relatives. The brass lectern was given by the Grays. At the time of the Grays, the house stood in a park of about 30 acres and had a fine command of the view of the sea. Many village functions were held in the grounds including the celebrations of Edward VII's Coronation when all the village children and the old people were entertained in the park.

The Friends are buried in a vault, in the north west part of the Church, where there are memorials on the wall. There is also a window in the Nave in memory of John Friend. The Friends farmed extensively in the area.

The house was sold by public auction in 1920, when it was bought by Spurgeons Homes to become the Spurgeons Seaside Homes for Children. It was demolished in 1967 as being unsuitable as a Home for small children. Later the site was developed into Birch Hill Park.

BIRCHINGTON HALL
Demolished in 1967

THE BERESFORD HOTEL AND GAP

Originally, this was the home of Major Morrison Bell and was known as Thor and Haun. Major Morrison Bell was an esteemed resident of Birchington and a most generous benefactor to the place. Morrison Bell House in Albion Road was erected in his memory. At the end of the last century it became the stately seaside home of Admiral Lord Charles William de la Poer Beresford, 4th Marquis of Waterford. He was a distinguished sailor and statesman and for many years was Naval A.D.C. to Queen Victoria. He was Commander in Chief of the Mediterranean and the Channel Fleets and at one time an M.P. for Waterford, Woolwich, and Portsmouth. He entertained quite lavishly at Birchington. He died without heir.

From Lord Beresford comes the name Beresford Lodge and Beresford Gap. The gap is man made.

During the First World War, Beresford Lodge became a British Red Cross Military Hospital.

Later, the Beresford Lodge became the plush 5 star Beresford Hotel, popular with political and entertainment celebrities including Sir Harold Wilson, Petula Clark and the Beatles. In the 1960's bookings had reduced mainly as the motoring organisations withdrew their recommendation. In 1967, the hotel closed and later in 1971, the site was sold and the six acre cliff site, overlooking the sea, was used for the building of houses.

In 1694, the Birchington Church owned much of the site, which was then let to a Henry Sprackling. In 1879, the Churchwardens at the time, Robert Edwards and Charles Moore, exchanged with William Morrison Bell, their piece of land of about 1½ acres for about 2¾ acres on the west side of Minnis Road, opposite the Malt House.

THE BAY HOTEL and UNCLE TOM'S CABIN

This was built in 1905 and was a well known hotel in Birchington. It was demolished in 1964 for the building of high rise flats.

MORRISON BELL HOUSE, ALBION ROAD

This house was built in memory of Major Morrison Bell as a Convalescent Home for delicate children from London. Major Bell died in 1900 and there is a plaque, to his memory, in the Parish Church. The house was seriously damaged by a bomb on the night of 6th August 1941, when the southern end of the house was demolished. After the war it was repaired to become flats and then sold to be demolished so that houses could be built on the site.

MORRISON BELL HOUSE
Albion Road

ST. MARY'S CONVALESCENT HOME, BEACH AVENUE

This home was built in 1882 as a sea-side home for mothers and babies from London. During the First World War it was used for a short time for wounded Belgian soldiers. Later it became a Convalescent Home for women and girls suffering from Diabetes and became known as St. Mary's Diabetic Home. It had a small chapel which was used nearly every week. The home was closed in 1971 and the building sold by the Thanet Hospital Management Committee. St. Mary's was one of two special units in the country which took in convalescent diabetics. It is now a private Old People's Home.

The following cottages and houses have been demolished in comparatively recent years:—

The **FLINT COTTAGES** in Gas Row.

BATH COTTAGES — Station Road at the junction with Albion Road. These cottages had a Dutch gable at the Albion Road end. Next to these, now where the Westminster Bank stands, was a thatched cottage and small cottage occupied by a chimney sweep and where fish and chips were sold.

CHAPEL PLACE — Canterbury Road, on the site of the Wesleyan Chapel, behind Southdown House.

POINT COTTAGES — Epple Bay, situated on the cliff top, demolished in 1938.

YEW TREE HOUSE — Canterbury Road, where Mrs. Perfect lived, demolished to become the Yew Tree Estate.

BARTLETTS COTTAGES — Albion Road, now an open space next to the Old Primitive Chapel, now demolished.

IVY COTTAGES — Canterbury Road. Demolished to become the Smugglers' car park.

WAYSIDE CAFE — Station Road. Noted for its large wooden swinging parrots in the forecourt. Demolished to become the Midland Bank and Woolworths, then the Co-op shop.

THE ALMSHOUSES — Park Lane, there were four almshouses, thatched.

THE SEED MILL — Close to the Railway Station, a few yards north of the Bridge. Referred to as a wind mill in the Tithe Map and owned by Lady Isabella Bridges.

THE OLD SHOPS — Station Road, next to the Westminster Bank. One was a Baker's and had the only brick oven in Thanet.

THE TOWER — Canterbury Road, across the field opposite Birchington Hall (now Birch Hill) and owned by John "Birchington" Friend.

THE WIND MILL — At the top of Mill Row. Often called Hudson's Mill. Now a private house.

*THE BUNGALOW HOTEL
Lyell Road, built about 1880*

BIERCE COURT, LYELL ROAD

Bierce Court is built on the site of the old Bungalow Hotel, the last of the three Birchington hotels to be demolished and the sites developed for the building of flats and houses. The Bungalow Hotel was designed by a Mr. John Taylor on the estate owned by a Mr. J. P. Seddon in about 1880 which included the Rossetti Bungalow and the Indian type bungalows built in Spencer Road. In Birchington were built the first bungalows of Great Britain. At first the Bungalow Hotel was known as the West Cliffe Hotel. It was quite large and commodious and built mainly of timber. There were no stairs, all the rooms being on one floor. Many local functions were held at this hotel.

THE THICKET, CROSS ROAD

The Thicket Convalescent Home was situated at the west end of Cross Road, at the junction with Coleman's Stairs Road and Epple Bay Road. It was built in 1900 by a Dr. Cross as a convalescent home and given to the Parish of St. Michael's, Chester Square, London for the poor parishioners of that parish, and so was sometimes known as St. Michael's Home. As it was built during the Boer War of 1900-1901, it was given over to the Household Cavalry as a convalescent home for wounded cavalry men as Dr. Cross's brother was the Colonel.

The first matron was a Miss Denning, who was matron for 31 years. She was the aunt of that well known character and animal lover of Birchington, Miss Denning. She was followed by a Mrs. Hiscock who was matron until 1948 and then by Mrs. Wiggens who remained until 1967 when the home was closed and later sold and demolished when the present houses were built on the site.

During the First World War it was used as a Hospital again by the Household Cavalry and then in 1916 for the Imperials until 1919. It had 30 beds. During the Second World War it was used by the military for billetting soldiers. The Vicar of St. Michael's, the Rev. Canon James Fleming resided at Erin Dene, Shakespeare Road when he retired in 1903.

Cross Road is named after Dr. Cross.

FERNDALE COURT, CANTERBURY ROAD

This development of 40 flats and Warden's Bungalow is built on the site of Church Hill Farm and Homestead, which was built probably in the late 1600s. The Farm is shown on the 1688 map of Birchington and as a Homestead on the Tithe Map of 1841. In 1841 it was owned by Lady Isobella Brydges who owned a number of properties in the village including the Seed Mill which stood near the railway station. The farm was then tenanted by Edward Neame and Kent Gardens opposite was then just a trackway leading towards Minnis Bay. In the 1950s the house and land were used as a builders storage. In about 1970 the house was demolished and the flats for the elderly constructed. The original house had Flemish bond brickwork suggesting that it dated from about 1680. The 1688 map of Birchington showing Church Hill Farm house and Homestead was made for John Bridges of Canterbury who had purchased the farm. The map was made by Thomas Hill, a surveyor. On the edge of the map near "Epald Baye" is the outline of a whale. The stranding of whales in the shallow coastal waters of Thanet is not infrequent. In 1914 a whale was stranded at Grenham Bay and the huge bones from this whale now form an archway in the garden of the Sea View Hotel.

STATION ROAD — about 1900 — from the bottom end looking to the Square, with Dog Acre on the left. Note the trees

THE BUNGALOWS OF BIRCHINGTON

Birchington and possibly, Westgate-on-Sea, have the distinction of being the first places in England to have bungalows.

The word bungalow comes from India and by the end of the 19th century the word was used to describe almost all single storey dwellings, occupied by Europeans in India. The credit for the introduction of the modified Indian hill country houses into England, goes to Mr. John Taylor and Mr. J. P. Seddon, an architect and builder. These two together, at first, were involved in this area as early as 1870, on land that apparently Seddon owned. In an article in the "Building News" of 1870, on "Sundry Works in the Isle of Thanet" mention is made of an estate of "considerable extent", laid out by a Mr. C. N. Beazley. He was an architect living in Westgate and designed the Church of St. Mildred at Acol, and also the Victorian oak screen that separated the Nave from the Chancel in the Birchington Parish Church and which was removed in 1968.

Mr. Erasmus Wilson, a famous surgeon at the time, bought one of Taylor's bungalows at Westgate and it was he who recommended Birchington's health giving air and so attracted clients to "a stretch of coast which was bleak and uninteresting and to the houses which had nothing between them and the sea, and nothing between them and the North Pole."

John Taylor erected several houses at Westgate and then moved westwards to Birchington where he continued to build Bungalows completely furnished. By 1880 it appears that Taylor dropped out of the partnership with Seddon and it is Seddon who is now referred to as the architect and owner of the land in Birchington. It was Seddon who built the Bungalow Hotel at first called the West Cliffe Hotel, then the Station Hotel — which catered for the increasing numbers brought by the railway.

Athol Mayhew, in his booklet "Birchington-on-Sea" which is really to boost Birchington and its Bungalows says, "Birchington-on-Sea is at its best when it is the dead season in London, during the Long Vacation, nowhere is to be found a cooler, healthier or more bracing retreat from the fierce autumnal heat which sears our southern coast." He further says, "At such times Birchington, on account of its northern aspect and the open character of the surrounding country, affords a breezy haven and cool retreat, the like of which is not to be found in any other watering place within the same distance of London." He calls the village of Birchington "The Village of Hygeia."

It seems as if Birchington was the first to have these Indian country houses in England because of its closeness to London, the railway had recently been extended to Birchington and Thanet and because of its bracing health giving air.

Seddon claimed that his bungalows were healthy and absolutely damp proof, the roofs all in one span with wide overhanging eaves, and all the rooms were on the ground floor. They had a long corridor with rooms opening on either side to the passage. He produced a large number of drawings — in fact some 2000 now in the Victoria and Albert Museum in London and some were designs for buildings at Birchington. Seddon produced a plan of Birchington showing how he proposed to develop the site near and around the bungalows already built by Taylor. Seddon planned a cliff estate along what is now Berkeley Road and Cliff Road, with bungalows facing the sea and stables behind. Unfortunately many of these were never built.

Seddon also planned and built two hotels, one later to become the Beresford Hotel and the other the Westcliff Hotel, later to be known as the Bungalow Hotel. But it seems as if this hotel was not built to Seddon's original design.

The Tower Bungalows, in Spencer Road, were designed and built by J. P. Seddon although all did not have towers and the original design had terraces down to the sea but these were never constructed, probably because the cliff face was much higher and steeper than thought.

Seddon himself lived in "Rossetti" Bungalow, which was mainly of wood constructed with asphelte roof with brick flues and chimney stacks. The bungalow had a lounge, a dining room, a study, 6 bedrooms, a front entrance hall, cellar and domestic offices.

Some of Seddon's buildings were ornamented by graffite work, work done by George Frampton, later to become Sir George Frampton, the eminent Victorian sculptor. It was he who designed the Peter Pan statue in Kensington Gardens.

On the "Porch" in Spencer Road can be seen graffite decoration and the words, "Ye Tower Bungalows 1882" also "J. P. Seddon Arch."

Other artists have lived at Birchington including Sir Alfred Gilbert, the sculptor who lived in Rossetti's bungalow in the mid 1880's and Solomon J. Solomon, R.A., also lived at Birchington for a time and had a studio in the cliff side.

Some of the houses in Spencer Road have interesting names, "Dilkoosha" or Hearts Delight, "Orion" derives its name from the atronomically correct representation of that constellation in a blue and gold morning room.

THE BIRCHINGTON WITH ACOL CHARITIES

As a result of the generosity and foresight of a few of Birchington's forbears, the village now has several charities. They are:—
1. The Crispe Charity — otherwise the Crispe's School and Exhibition Foundation.
2. The Robinson, Jennings, Friend and Williamson Charity.
3. The Birchington Institute Trust.
4. The Church Lands Charity.
5. The Emma Simmons Charity — for Acol.
6. The Old Scholars' Club — otherwise known as the Band Room.

THE CRISPE CHARITY

This charity dates from 1708 when Mistress Anna Gertruy Crispe, fourth and youngest daughter and co-heir of Thomas Crispe of Quex bequeathed to the Overseers of the Poor of the Parish of Birchington and Ville of Acole, 47 acres of farmland, now known as the Crispe Farm, the income from which should be used to improve the lot of poor widows of Birchington and Acol and for education. The Parish Church Verger was also to receive a yearly payment of 20s for "to keep clean the aisle and monuments belonging to Quex." This means the Quex Chapel.

Under the terms of the original will, a summary of which can be seen on her monument in the Quex Chapel, three poor windows of Birchington and two of the Ville of Acol are to have "each of them twenty shillings at Christmas, to be laid out in wearing apparel for their better appearing at Church, which the Overseers are to see observed." The balance of the income was to be used to maintain at School "with an able Dame or Schoolmaster" 12 boys and girls, to be taught and learn to read and write and the girls to "worke Neddleworke", and to apprentice boys to some handicraft trade.

As a result, the Crispe Charity School came into existence in Birchington in 1709 and remained in existence for well over a hundred years.

In 1862, the Scheme for the Regulation and Management of the Charity was revised and approved by the Master of the Rolls. No change was made in the payment to the five widows or to the Verger but the Trustees were empowered either to pay up to £50 a year towards the maintenance of the National Schools in Park Lane or to maintain their own school in Birchington. Boys could still be apprenticed to some handicraft trade.

In 1879, the Scheme regulating the Charity was again revised by an Order approved by her Majesty Queen Victoria in Council. Again the original bequests to the 5 widows and the verger were not altered but the residue of the income of the charity was for the future to be divided into 3 equal parts. Two parts were to be applied to the support of the public elementary schools in Birchington and Acol and one part for exhibitions to a higher grade school or in apprenticing boys and girls.

Again, in 1957 the Scheme regulating the Charity was revised but again, no change was allowed to the original bequests to the 5 widows and the verger. Now that the Schools in Park Lane were under the control of the Kent County Council as a Controlled Church of England School, grants were no longer made to the School so the income could now be used for making grants to young people starting out on their careers, and also to assist Youth Organisations promoting the education including the social and physical training of young people.

In 1978, the Charity Commissioners again revised the Scheme regulating the Charity to modernise it and at the same time to keep within the original intention of the donor, specially as the income is now considerably increased.

When the charity was first instituted, the income was about £18 a year and the population in 1708 was about 275. Now the income is over £1,000 a year and the population over 10,000.

Under this new scheme, a yearly payment of £28 is made to the Church Parochial Council of the Parish of Birchington towards the upkeep and maintenance of the Quex Chapel, £139 a year can be used to relieve the widows of Birchington and Acol who, in the opinion of the Governors, are in condition of need, hardship or distress, and the residue can be used in promoting the education, including social and physical training of persons under 25 years who are resident in the area of benefit.

The present Governors are, beside the Vicar of the Parish who is ex-officio:—

  2 appointed by the Acol Parish Council
  1 appointed by the Education Committee of the Kent County Council
  4 Co-optative Governors — persons resident in the area of benefit, who have special knowledge of the area.

The Charity still owns the Crispe Farm of 47 acres and has some money invested.

In 1990, several young people starting out on their careers were given financial assistance as well as organisations catering for the welfare of the young people of this place.

THE ROBINSON, JENNINGS, FRIEND AND WILLIAMSON CHARITY

This charity is a combination of three charities and regulated by a scheme drawn up by the Charity Commissioners in 1952.

The Henry Robinson Charity dates from 1642 when Henry Robinson, gent, left by will five acres of arable land in the Parish of St. Lawrence called by the name of Fleet Close, and five acres of meadow ground in the Parish of Chislet towards the relief of four widows exceeding the age of three score years, two of which to be of the Parish of Monkton and the other two of the Parish of Birchington. In 1896, the Charity Commissioners separated the Birchington from the Monkton part of the Charity but the property of the original charity is to be managed by the Trustees of the Charity in the Parish of Monkton.

The Sarah Jennings and Elizabeth Friend Charity dates from 1826. These two ladies, relatives of Mr. John Friend of Birchington Hall, later Spurgeons Homes, bequeathed some land near Colemans Stairs and £200 for the benefit of the poor of Birchington. Later the land was sold and with the £200, the nett balance was invested by the Charity Commissioners in Consols.

The Trustees are the Vicar of the Ecclesiastical Parish of Birchington with Acol and four representative Trustees appointed by the local Council. After expenses have been defrayed, the yearly income is devoted for the benefit of such poor persons resident in the area of the Ancient Parish of Birchington.

THE BIRCHINGTON INSTITUTE TRUST

When the old Institute in the Square was sold in 1952, the nett proceeds were invested by the Charity Commissioners and a scheme established to regulate it as a charity. According to the scheme, the Trustees shall apply the income for any charitable purposes for the benefit of the inhabitants of Birchington not provided out of rates, taxes or other public funds. There are five Trustees appointed by the local Council, competent persons residing in Birchington.

THE CHURCH LANDS CHARITY

This is a Church Charity dating from "time immemorial". The Church at Birchington has owned land and other property for many centuries, and much of the land owned to-day by the Church has been in possession of Birchington Church for several hundreds of years. The Administrative Trustees are the Vicar of the Parish, the Churchwardens and the Birchington Parochial Church Council.

The clear income of the Charity shall be applied by the Managing Trustees in or towards defraying the cost of repairing and beautifying the Parish Church and in so far as the yearly income is not required for this purpose, the Trustees may apply the same in furthering the religious and other charitable work of the Church of England in the ecclesiastical parish of Birchington with Acol.

THE MRS. EMMA SIMMONS CHARITY

In 1921, Mrs. Emma Simmons of Ramsgate, bequeathed the sum of £100 to the Vicar and Churchwardens of Birchington to invest and apply the income in the distribution of coal among the poor in the parish of Acol. The Charity Commissioners invested the money and the Official Trustee of Charitable Funds remits the income each half year to the bank.

THE OLD SCHOLARS' CLUB
otherwise known as the Band Room, Park Lane

This is now a registered charity. The Club was formed in 1928 for the physical, social and educational welfare of the old scholars of the Birchington Church of England Boys School in Park Lane. The Club was formed by Mr. C. Laming the then Headmaster of the school.

A piece of land on the east side of Park Lane was purchased from Major Powell Cotton and on this land the old scholars built their own club house. For some years the building was used by the old boys of the School, the Club being managed by elected old boys of the school. Since the Second World War, several attempts were made to run a Club for boys but unfortunately all failed. The Committee of Management then let the building and applied the income from this letting to the furtherance of Youth Activities in the Parish of Birchington and Acol.

The objects of the Charity, as set out by the Charity Commissioners are:—

> To help the youth of Birchington and Acol, especially but not exclusively through leisure-time activities, so as they develop their physical, mental and spiritual capacities that they may grow to full maturity as individuals and members of society.

The nett income is distributed to the various youth organisations of Birchington and Acol. The annual income is about £50.

At present the building is let to the Birchington Band.

BIRCHINGTON IN THE MID 19th CENTURY —

EXTRACTS FROM THE AUTOBIOGRAPHY OF MR. THOMAS JAMES POINTER

Readers will find the following extracts from the Life Story of Mr. T. J. Pointer, who lived in Birchington well over 100 years ago, describing his humble life pattern, his family and Birchington as it was during the reign of Queen Victoria, very interesting.

He writes, "This Book contains a short history of my life and its surroundings together with some items of the three Parishes in which I have lived, namely, Birchington, Margate and St. Peters, the latter in which I have lived since 1858. It is not my intention to write anything that I have done either good or bad, for I feel that I have not done much that is worthy to be left on record and I know that there has been in my life much that has been wrong, much that is known only to God and myself for which I believe that God for Christ's sake has forgiven me. It is not my intention in writing this history to have it published, the object is that my children, should they survive me, may have something to remember me after I have passed away. The History dates back to the year of Human Redemption 1837 to the year 1912.

In a cottage, No. 2 Chapel Yard (1), at Birchington, on Friday, February 10th 1837 (2), I first saw the light. It was the year which followed the terrific November gale which did so much damage on land and sea, and which was followed by one of the severest winters on record. It set in on Christmas Eve 1836 and lasted till the following March.

I was born of humble parents, true and sincere, Christians both of them, who strove by the help of God, both by their teaching and in their lives to bring up their children in the fear of the Lord. My father was the third son of the late Jarvis Pointer of Birchington (3) who died when I was about four or five years of age. My Grandmother died in 1843. They had a large family to bring up and the times they lived in were hard and provisions were very dear, even rough meal was a guinea per bushel. I have heard my father say that to taste a piece of meat was almost a thing unknown. Just a plain dumpling and a few potatoes in the week and a red herring on Sunday, and for supper go and find a swede turnip field, pull one up, peel it and eat it. The law was not so strict on that sort of thing as it is now.

My dear mother was the eldest daughter of the late Thomas Hughes of Acol. His occupation was that of a shepherd and my dear mother, who was his favourite daughter, often went with him to tend the sheep. My father was born on the 21st March 1795 (4), my mother April 28th 1800 (5). They were married in the Old Church at Birchington in the year 1819 (6) and never lived out of the village afterwards. My mother died October 8th 1852, my father April 22nd 1866. They rest in peace. They were both Wesleyans, but very broad-minded, they could worship in any other place of worship, Church included. Often, when I was quite young, my father would take me with him into the old Church Porch on Sunday mornings in the summer time and sit on the seat, there used to be one on each side, and listen to the sermon and if the door was shut, he would listen through the keyhole. My father was a very quiet man in every way, he never made a noise of his religion. He was quiet in the home and as quiet at his work amongst his mates but he would always stand up for what was just and right in the sight of God and man. My dear mother was the same in every way. They both lived quiet Christian lives and now, without doubt, they are enjoying the rest that remains for the people of God.

They had five children, three sons and two daughters. I am the only surviving one, how soon I shall be called to join them, God alone knows. My eldest brother was born on the 1st of September 1820, and was named Robert (7), and lived to the age of 86. He married Mary Reynolds of Eastry by whom he had five children, one son and four daughters. My eldest sister was born on the 3rd April 1822 and was named Elizabeth (8) and lived to be just over 80. She married George Carter of Chislet where they lived all their married life.

They had a family of twelve children, 8 boys and 4 girls of whom 9 are living. My other brother was born 27th February 1842 (9) and was named Henry and lived to the age of 72. He married Rachel the eldest daughter of the late Edward Brockman of Brooksend in the Parish of Birchington. They also had a family of 12 children, 8 boys and 4 girls of whom 7 are living at present. My youngest sister was born on the 12th January 1839 and was named Sarah Ann. She lived to be just over 4 years. She was afflicted from her birth. She could neither walk nor talk nor even sit down in a chair without being tied in. It was a happy release when God in His mercy, took her to Himself. I can well remember her birth although not quite two years old, something took place at the time which I have never forgotten.

I was baptized in the old Church on Sunday April 9th (10), by the Curate in charge, the Rev. Edward Green and lived in the cottage in which I was born until I left it to go out into the world to earn my own living in October 1853. But although I had left the dear old home I could always go there until the year 1887 when it passed out of the family. Now I feel that I should like to go there once more and be left alone for one short hour and sit and think of the days gone by never to return. The scenes and memories of my childhood would come back to me with greater force than they could anywhere else. I can picture the dear old rooms, four in number. I seem to see the living room furnished as it was then, every chair and table and the position in which they stood. I can see my dear mother move about the house doing her work or sitting in her chair sewing, especially on a winter's evening and my father the other side and myself in front of them on a stool, reading, for they would never allow me to run the streets as the boys do now. I can see my father sitting in his chair, enjoying a nap or perhaps he would be repairing his flail which he used in threshing the corn, there were no threshing machines in those days. I can picture myself standing at the window to watch for his coming home and often in the evening I would climb on his knee before I was put to bed and he would sing hymns to me. One of Dr. Watts', was a great favourite of his — Come all harmonious Tongues."

Mr. Pointer now goes on to describe his school days, the Church and Birchington in 1850.

"My father never went to the public house to spend his evenings, he was too fond of his home for that. I can see myself watching the snow coming gently down and at Christmas time, listening to the old Church bells as they rang out the joyous message of the Saviour's birth. And then again in the Spring, I would watch the martins build their nests under the eaves of the roof of the Chapel windows, where they used to come every year and as soon as they got their nest built, the sparrows would come and turn them out. But the man that lived next door to us had a gun and he used to shoot at them and drive them away. Now I was always afraid of a gun and so when I found that he was about to fire it off, I used to run to dear mother for protection. Dear mother, I can see her now with arms around me, sheltering me and telling me not to be afraid. But the sparrows and the men with the gun are all gone and I am left.

Now I must pass on to my School days. The first School I went to was kept by an old lady by the name of Darby, the widow of a smuggler and lived in a cottage at the west end of the Churchyard (11). She used to take in young children to keep them out of their mother's way for a few hours. She could not learn them much for she did not know much herself. Then when I was old enough to learn to spell and read and write, I went to a house, No. 2 Brunswick Row, where a Coastguard lived by the name of Davis whose wife kept a School, and there I learned to read and write and soon made progress. I stayed there until I was old enough to go into the Village School (12). The Master's name was Thomas Sidders (13). His wife and daughter used to teach the girls. Here I remained until I left School. My parents paid 6d per week for me until there was a vacancy for me in the Charity School (14), which was in the same building and conducted by the same Master, who received his salary from the Trustees of the late Ann Gertrude Crispe of Quex Park who died March 23rd 1708 (15). She was buried in the Quex Vault in the Church who left in her will, provision for 12 boys and girls to be educated free for 3 years and each one to receive a Bible when they left school. I do not seem to remember whether I stayed the whole three years, at all events I did not get a Bible.

The National School was built in the end of the forties but I did not go to it. It was built on the side of the old Workhouse, along the road leading to Quex Park, at the far end of Brunswick Row. The first Schoolmaster's name was Paul Allard (16).

When I was old enough to commence work, it was on the farm where my father worked for over forty years. It was Brooksend Farm, one of the farms belonging to Canterbury Cathedral. The occupier was the late John Friend, Esq., who died in July 1862 and was buried in the family vault in the west end of the Church (17). At first I only went in the Spring and Summer when there was weeding to do among the corn. There used to be quite a string of us with a man to look after us and I can assure you we wanted looking after. It took him all his time to keep us in order. Then there was haymaking in the fields and the marshes and then we were done until the next year. Then, after a year or two, I became a regular work boy and continued on the farm until I left home to go to service, on the 15th October 1853. My pay was 6d per day and from that day, I have never set foot on the dear old farm.

I should like to have a peep at it just as it was when I left it. I seem to remember every part of it, the barns and stables, the graneries, the cow sheds and pigsties and the pond around which grew high poplar trees and the old pump which stood at the back of the farm house and the waggon and cart lodges and several other sheds which stood just outside the farm yard. But I could not see it as it was then, for most of the buildings were destroyed by fire several years ago. In fact, almost very farm in Thanet has been either totally or partly destroyed by fire, within the last fifty years.

Before I go on to speak of my life after I left home, I will give a short account of Birchington as it was when I lived in it. I will begin with the Church. I can give no account of the date of the year when it was built but in the Church there is a slab in the pavement on the north side of the Chancel on which is recorded the death of John Quex, who died in October 1449 (18). So it must be a very ancient building. I can remember the old high backed pews and the three decker pulpit and the sounding board over head and a gallery at the west end (19). In former years, the living went with Monkton where the Vicar lived, and before he kept a

Curate he used to have one service at each Church on a Sunday, one week he would have Morning Service at Monkton and come to Birchington for the afternoon Service. The next Sunday he would come over to Birchington in the morning and go back to Monkton for the afternoon Service. But that was before my time, for as I mentioned in the early part of this history it was the Curate who baptized me. The Curate who was there when I left home was the Rev. Henry Wish, the son of the Vicar the Rev. Peter Wish, who was the last Vicar who held both livings. The Rev. Alcock was the first Vicar after the livings were divided (20).

The Wesleyan Chapel was built in 1830. The ground and the Tower and the Clock were given by the late William Tomlin, Esq., whose son is now one of the Guardians of the Poor.

There were 3 Public Houses, the Powell Arms, The New Inn and the Acorn. Now there are 5 (21). There were two Groceries Shops, two Butchers Shops, two Carpenters Shops and two Blacksmiths Forges, a Tailors Shop and a Drapers Shop and three Bootmakers Shops and one or two sweet shops. There was no Chemist or Doctor living in the Village. The nearest doctor lived at Minster 3 miles off or Margate which is 4 miles. There was only one post in the day. The Postman that brought the letters came from Margate reaching Birchington at eight in the morning, leave the letters at the Post Office and then go on to St. Nicholas, do the same there and then go on to Sarre, and remain there until the evening and then return to Birchington reaching there at half past six and pick up letters and go on to Margate. If he had any letters from Sarre or St. Nicholas for Birchington, he would take them on to Margate and bring them back the next morning."

Mr. Pointer continues his description of Birchington, describes the funeral of John Powell Powell of Quex and his removal to Garlinge.

"The old Village Fair used to be held on Whit Monday and Tuesday, when stalls for the sale of nuts, oranges, gingerbreads and other sorts of cakes and sweets used to be erected in front of the Church wall, also coconut shieing and other sports would take place. Dancing in the Public Houses would go on nearly the whole night but these things have all passed away, and a very good thing too, for there was sure to be a row before it was over and very often a fight. Birchington Square is one of the largest in Thanet. It used to be a green but that was before my time. It was there where we boys used to play our games such as Bat Ball, Rounder, Leap Frog, Marbles and various other games. Cricket and Football were not known to us then.

There were not many Gentry in the Village. There was Mr. George Friend, who had Brooksend Farm and lived in a house opposite the

Chancel of the Church, where he died in 1862. There were two maiden ladies by the name of Neame (22). John P. Powell lived at Quex Park and died in May 1849, and had a grand funeral (23). There were a great number of people at the funeral, the Street was crowded, in fact it was more like a fair than a funeral. There were oyster barrows, barrows with nuts and oranges, ginger beer at different parts of the Street. It was a large procession, all the working men from the different farms had a half day off to come and see it. I remember it well. It was a bitter cold day in May. In front of the procession came a man carrying on his head a board covered with large black plumes, behind him walked a large number of men belonging to the Philanthropic Society. Then came the hearse drawn by 6 black horses. The top of the hearse was covered with black plumes and then followed 9 or 11, I forget, of the old fashioned mourning coaches, some with four horses and some with two. Every horse had a black cloth on its back and a plume on its head. All the black horses from the farms were hired for the occasion and whatever horse had a white mark was covered with some black composition. Then followed the Esquires Carriages. Then came the private carriages of the Gentry round about the Island. When they took the coffin out of the drawing room at Quex Park, a cannon fired as many times as he was years old, 84. I did not go into the vault for there was too great a crowd of people but I can remember my mother taking me with her to look down into it a few years before, when it was opened for Lady Powell who died at Fulham in the month of August. But I do not know the date of the year (24).

The vault is on the north side of the Chancel and under the Quex Pew, which in my time at Birchington was a square platform several feet high, with steps leading up to it. But the last time that I went into the Church, I found that it had been lowered to the level of the Chancel floor (25). It is a very ancient vault as you will find it mentioned in the earlier part of this history. Several of the Cottons, late of the Convent of Kingsgate, are buried in it.

After the death of the Squire, Henry Cotton, son of the late Captain Cotton of Kingsgate, took possession of Quex with his wife and family (26). His eldest son, Horace, came of age in January 1850. There were great festivities at Quex on that day. His brother, George, became his mother's coachman and after staying at the Park a few months, the whole family went away and the old people never came back, at least I never heard that they did. The estate was then let to tennants until Horace came to it again and ended his days there and was buried in the family vault and lay there for two years when his son, the present Major Powell Cotton of Quex, returned from India and had a tomb built in the Park, near the Bell Tower and having procured a Faculty removed his father from the vault by night and placed him in the new tomb at Quex.

There were two windmills at Birchington, both of which have disappeared. One of them was a flour mill between the village of Brooksend (27), and the other, a seed mill, which stood between the L.C.D. Railway and the sea opposite the station (28). In the year 1850, a large whale was caught off Margate and the skeleton was riveted together and a shed was erected on the Fort, near the Pier, where it was exhibited for a long time. The charge for admission was one penny. About the same time a large eagle was caught off Broadstairs, by a man named Sandwich, who had a large cage made for it and he took it round from place to place for exhibition, the charge being one penny. I remember seeing it at Birchington, in the Parish Lane.

On the 8th October, 1852, the greatest misfortune happened to me that can happen to a lad of my age. I lost my precious mother, who passed away at half past three in the afternoon. I was not present nor yet my father or sister but I think my two brothers were. Her suffering was very greatly caused by a bleeding cancer in her neck. She was buried on the 10th October, in the old Churchyard. My father was laid in the same grave on April 28th 1866. They lie between the path and the wall opposite the Chancel. My father and I lived alone until the next February, when my brother Henry and his wife gave up their cottage and came to live with us. Then on the 15th October 1853, I left the dear old home and went out in the world to earn my living."

Mr. Pointer then goes on to describe how he went to live and work on a farm at Garlinge, he describes some events which he remembered when he was there, the visit of the Archbishop of Canterbury to St. John's Church, Margate, the building of the new jetty at Margate, the wreck of the Northern Belle in 1857, the capsizing of the Victory Lugger and the drowning of nine Margate crew, his marriage and his removal to St. Peter's, and his life in that place.

NOTES

1. Chapel Yard is the plot of ground on the east side of the Wesleyan Chapel. Three cottages, known as Chapel Cottages, stood there. They were demolished some years ago.
2. From the Parish Baptism Register:—
1837 Apr 9 Thomas James, son of Thomas and Sarah Pointer, Labourer.
3. From the Parish Baptism Register:—
1762 Aug 1st Jarvis son Wm and Elizabeth Pointer.
4. From the Parish Baptism Register:—
1795 Pointer Thomas of Jarvis and Sarah May 3.
5. From the Parish Baptism Register:—
1799 Hughes Sarah dr. of Thomas and Mary May 26th.

6. From the Marriages Register:—
   1818 Oct 13 Thomas Pointer and Sarah Hughes — (both signed by mark.)
7. There is no record of the Baptism in the Register.
8. From the Baptism Register:—
   1822 Apr 28th Elizabeth daughter of Thomas and Sarah Pointer. Labourer.
9. From the Baptism Register:—
   1824 Apr 11th Henry son of Thomas and Sarah Pointer. Labourer.
10. See note 2.
11. The cottage is no longer in existence. It was part of Street Farm. The site now forms part of the Churchyard.
12. The first Village School and Charity School, was near the junction of Park Road and Canterbury Road.
13. A Thomas Sidders was also a Churchwarden for many years.
14. See the section on the Charity School.
15. Anna Gertruy Crispe was the founder of the Crispe Charity. See the section on the Crispe Charity.
16. Paul Allard was also Overseer of the Poor in 1858.
17. There is a memorial tablet to John Friend of Brooksend on the north wall of the Nave towards the west. The vault is beneath. The tablet says he died July 4th 1858.
18. The memorial brass to John Quex is now on the north wall of the Quex Chapel.
19. The pews and gallery were removed at the restoration of the Church in 1864 and the pulpit placed in its present position at the same time.
20. Birchington was separated from the ecclesiastical parish of Monkton in 1871. The Rev. John Price Alcock, M.A., was the first Vicar of Birchington.
21. The Queen's Head must have been there as it is mentioned in the Kentish Gazette in 1768.
22. There is a mural tablet on the south wall of the Church between the south door and the Rossetti window to the Neame family, with the names Charlotte Neame and Maria Neame, both daughters of John Neame. Charlotte died in 1872 aged 79 years, and Maria in 1879 aged 91 years.
23. John Powell Powell died at Quex 14th May 1849 aged 79 years and was buried in the Quex vault. There is a white sarcophagus with drapery and coat of arms on the west wall of the Chapel, above the arch, to the memory of John Powell Powell and his wife Charlotte.
24. Charlotte Powell Powell died in 1844.
25. The Quex Pew, a raised pew somewhat like an opera box in the Chapel, blocked the whole of the first arch between the Chancel and the Chapel. It was approached by steps from the north aisle of the Nave which covered the entrance to the Quex Vault. This raised pew was taken down at the Victorian restoration of 1863.
26. Henry Perry Cotton was the nephew of John Powell Powell. He died in 1881 when the Quex estate passed to his son Henry Horace Powell Cotton.
27. This mill stood at the end of Mill Lane. Some flints from this Mill were used in the building of the new Vestries in 1909. The Seed Mill was opposite the Bungalow Hotel.
28. This is the old London, Chatham and Dover Railway which first came to Birchington in 1863.

THE CHURCH OF
ST. NICHOLAS AT WODE - WOODCHURCH

Not many people of Birchington or Acol know that once there was a large Church at Woodchurch, known as the church of St. Nicholas at Wode. At one time its foundations could be seen in the ground opposite Woodchurch Farm House.

It is this Church of St. Nicholas at Wode which is refered to in the Domesday Book of 1086, under the entry for "Moncstune" (Monkton) which included Woodchurch and Birchington, and was held by the Archbishop and the Monks of Christ Church, Canterbury. The Domesday Book states that there were two churches in Monkton, one of which was, of course, Monkton Church and the other probably St. Nicholas at Wode. The Domesday Book states that there was woodland for the pannage of 10 hogs (right of pasture for pigs on acorns and beech mast).

The Church must have been of considerable size as Hasted in his History of Kent 1797, states that the church must have been quite large as its foundations measured from east to west 84 feet and from north to south 56 feet, that is nearly as big as Birchington Church. The late Mrs. Powell Cotton estimated the foundations to measure some 86 feet by 80 feet but she did state that these measurements should be regarded with caution.

The walls were of rough flint and mortar and appeared to have an average width of 3 feet to 3 feet 6 inches. Some worked stones from the church can still be seen in the farm buildings on the opposite side of the road. Hasted says that the high road from Margate to Sarre and so the Canterbury, passed about a quarter of a mile or a little more to the north of the church ruins. In Hasted's time only parts of the walls were left and a mound of 8 or 10 feet high in the middle of the area of the Church which evidently appears to be the ruins of the tower, and the church yard surrounded by the original walls which had been converted into a meadow. Lewis in his "History of Tenet" 1737 says "only part of the walls are left and its yard converted into a lay fee."

The earliest known map of Thanet, made in 1414 by Thomas of Elmham, a monk and Treasurer of St. Augustine's Abbey, Canterbury, shows the church of Wodechurch" as one of the 13 churches in Thanet. It is represented by an oblong box in red with four windows picked out in blue surrounded by a red oblong with blue windows possibly to represent the tower with a steeple rising from it. Elmham possible represented the Church as it was with tower and steeple. Nearby, Elmham has marked a thick wood. The highway from St. Johns (Margate) to St. Giles (Sarre) runs near by.

On nearly all early 16th century maps of Kent, Woodchurch is marked. Symonson's map of Kent dated 1596, one of the earliest county maps and made when the Church was still standing marks Woodchurch "St. Nych at Wood" with a small drawing of a church with a tower and steeple.

The Church was dedicated to St. Nicholas, and was a dependent chapel of Monkton. A church must have been here in 1292, in the time of Edward I, for in that year the Parish priest of Wode was cited, with others, concerning the vacancy of the Church of Monkton. In 1377, Archbishop Langton decreed that the Vicar of Monkton, the mother church, should find a chaplain to celebrate in the chapel on Sundays, Wednesdays and Fridays and for this duty the priest was to be paid £3 14s 4d yearly.

By the beginning of the reign of Queen Elizabeth I, it seems as if the small hamlet of Woodchurch had so decayed that the church was no longer used and by about 1563, services in it were discontinued, and by the end of her reign the church was being pulled down and allowed to fall into ruin.

The names of several people buried in the Churchyard of St. Nicholas at Wood are known, obtained from Wills kept at Canterbury, such as Thomas Holwarding in 1497, Nicholas Palmer in 1527, Michael Burforth, John Helling and Thomas Burges in 1527, and Nicholas Coleman in 1544.

Inside the Church was a Rood with an image of the Blessed Mary, and an altar dedicated to St. James, and no doubt, at service times the church was quite brightly lit by candles. This is known from the Wills kept at Canterbury, and from which is learnt what was bequeathed by benefactors for the upkeep of the lights and altars.

In 1428, Cecilia Parker left 40d to the Light of the Blessed Mary in the Church of Woode. The Parkers preceded the Quex family at Quex and lived in a house called the Parkers near the present Quex mansion. The house is marked "Parker" on Thomas of Elmham's map of 1414. The same Cecilia also left 40d to the Light of the Torches of Woode.

In 1472, Thomas Smyth Philpott of St. John's in Thanet left 2 bushells of barley to the Light of St. Mary of Woode. In 1527, Nicholas Palmer besides directing to be buried in the Churchyard of St. Nicholas at Wood left a bushel of barley to the Light of St. Mary.

John Pettit, of Birchington, in 1523 left 2s 0d to the "reparacion of the Cross of St. Nicholas at Woode". In 1536, John Stretyn directed that he should be buried before the Altar of St. James in the Church of Woode.

One of the vicars of St. John's, John Bowrman in 1535, by his Will gave the residue of wax to Wodechurch in Thanet after giving one pound of wax to every Light in St. John's Thanet of which he was a brother.

Several people left money to go towards the upkeep of the Church. In 1414, John Parker left 10s 0d and Richard Quex in 1459, 3s 4d. A memorial brass to Richard Quex is on the wall of the Quex Chapel of Birchington Church.

A certain Kateryn Sheche bequeathed land for the fabric of the parish church of St. Nicholas at Woode for the relief of the poor and for a yearly mass to be said for the repose of his soul. A Nichol Chesterfelde also bequeathed land to the Church for masses for the repose of his soul. John Chestvyld in 1488 left land for the maintaining of the Pascal Taper. This land was sold at the Reformation in 1549.

In 1602, one Thomas Rowe of Birchington appeared in the Archdeacon's Court for pulling down the Church and the adjoining school house of Woodchurch. The Churchwardens stated that the "school house was erected for education and teaching of the young of our parish" and that "the said Church and School House are much and almost altogether ruinated and defaced." They alleged that Thomas Rowe pulled them down or parts of them to convert the same to private buildings. Rowe in defence stated he pulled down part of the school house "by the procurement of Mr. Henry Crispe (of Quex) and the stones used in the building of a house near to the Church." He said "the lead of the Church was pulled off and carried by his carts to Mr. Crispe's house called Quex." Rowe added that "about 3 or 4 years previously, Mr. Crispe then about to build a house near unto the Church of Woodchurch, the labourers which were used then to serve the masons gathered up some good quantity of stones which fell from the walls of the said church and the masons employed the said stones on the building aforesaid."

Woodchurch is in the ecclesiastical parish of Birchington.

It was in 1604 that the two parishes of Birchington and the Ville of Wood were united for ecclesiastical matters but kept separate for civil matters.

PROMENADE, MINNIS BAY
Birchington, early 1900's

Fred Castle — the last horse and cart in Birchington

BIBLIOGRAPHY

Parish of Birchington Churchwardens' Account Books — from 1531.

Parish of Birchington and Vill of Wood Poor Books — from 1611.

Birchington Paris Church Records — including the Registers from 1538.

Archaeologia Cantiana — The Transactions of the Kent Archaeological Society, 1858 to 1988.

Testamenta Cantiana — Extracts from 15th and 16th Century Wills, 1906.

History and Topographical Survey of the County of Kent, E. Hasted, 1797.

The History of the Isle of Tenet, John Lewis — 2nd Edition, 1736.

A History of the Ville of Birchington, Thanet, — J. P. Barrett, 1893.

Birchington-on-Sea. Athol Mayhew, 1881.

The Parish Chest. W. E. Tate, 1946.

The Kent Coast Blockade. R. Finn, 1971.

Log Books of the Birchington National Schools from 1863.

A Saunter through Kent with Pen and Pencil. Charles Igglesden, Vol. XXVII, 1933.

VILLE OF BIRCHINGTON : A. T. WALKER : 1990
INDEX

ACOL: 2 142
  (also Woodchurch)
ALPHA ROAD: 135
ALMSHOUSES: 73 74-81 154
  (also Workhouse : Poor)
ALTARS: 11 59-62
ALTAR RAILS: 44
APPRENTICES: 14 15 68 70
ARMADA SESS: 17
BAZAAR (1900): 96
BEACON: 131
BEDLEM COTTAGE: 131
BELLS: 9 14 45
BIRCHINGTON: 1 2 74 140
  (spelling)
BOUNDS: 9 120-122
  (beating)
BRASSES: 44 45
BRICKFIELDS: 5 23 131
BUILDING MATERIALS: 42-3
BUNGALOWS: 91 158-9
BUTTS: 134
CAGE: 16 19-20 55-57 87-91
  (inc. Jail, Stocks & Offenders)
CANDLES: 11 58 59-62
  (inc. Lights) (see also, Wax House)
CHAPELS: 45-50
CHARITIES: 14 92 93 133 160-163
CHURCH: 42-45
  (general description)
CHURCHWARDENS JOBS: 15-20
  "   ACCOUNTS: 7
CHURCHYARD: 73 75 115 118
CINQUE PORT: 15 22
  (Dover)
CLOCK: 102
CLOTHES: 66 70 72
COAST GUARDS: 17 23 115-119 131
COLEMAN'S STAIRS: 131
COMPOSITION MONEY: 6
COWS: 10
CRISPES: 26-38 60 97 102-104
  (inc. Quekes, Powell-Cotton)
CYCLE FACTORY: 131
DEPUTY (for Cinque Port): 15-20 53

DOCUMENTS: 6-14
DOG ACRE: 134-135
DOORS (North): 44
DOVER (see Deputy / Cinque Port)
EPPLE BAY: 131
ERLEBACH: 99
EROSION: 21
EXHIBITION: 23
FLOOR: 8 11
FOOD: 66 70 73 79-80 91
FOUNTAIN: 136-139
GAPS (in cliffs): 131
GAS LAMPS: 131
GORE END: 15 16 17 21 123 128 131
GREEN ROAD: 131
GRENHAM ROAD: 131
HEYNYS (see Vicars)
HISTORY (early): 3-5 164-171
HOCKTIDE: 58
HOTELS: 23 148 152 155
HOUSES: 5 23 91 143-157 (to let) 10
IMAGES: 59-62
INDENTURES: 14
INGOLDSBY LEGENDS: 119
INSTITUTE: 23 132 133
JESTON: 99
LANDS (Church): 14 16 (to let) 10
LIME KILNS: 131
KING'S ARMS: 11
  (Wooden panel hung in church)
LIGHTING: 11 62 131
  (see also Candles)
LYCH GATE: 99
MALT HOUSE: 128
MANSTON RAILWAY LINE: 141
MAP: 58
MAYPOLE: 58
MEASURES: 69 70
MEDICAL: 73
MILL: 128 155
MINNIS BAY: 23 123-131 141
MONKTON: 39-41
MONUMENTS: 45 115 118
MOTOR CARS: 131
NAMES: 16

NAVE: 43
OFFENDERS (see Cage)
ORGAN: 11
OVERSEERS: 56 116
  (see also Poor:)
PAINTING (of the Church): 11
PARISH COUNCIL: 99
  (see also Vestry Meetings)
PARISH CHEST: 11
PLAGUE: 7 63-67 86
POND: 128
POOR: LAW & BOOKS: 13 15 64-7 68-73 74-81 87 91
  (see also Workhouse and Almshouse)
POPULATION: 17 63-4 66 69 93
POST OFFICE: 23
POWELL-COTTON: 10
PUBS: 14 58 122 147 148
QUAKERS: 51-52
QUEEN BERTHA'S SCHOOL: 100
QUEEN EDIVA: 39
QUEKES (see Crispe)
QUEX PARK: 53-54 81 141
QUEX CHAPEL: 26 34 45 53
RAILWAY: 23 90 140-142
RECEIPTS: 6 10 16 17
RECREATION GROUND: 99
RECULVER: 21
REGISTERS: 6-7
RENTING (animals and property): 10 57
REREDOS: 11 44
RESTORATION (1863-4): 42
RIDING OFFICERS (see Coast Guards)
RIOTS: 87-91
  (see also Cage)
ROADS: 42 123 131 141
ROOD SCREEN & LOFT: 11 61
ROOF (Church): 44
ROSSETTI: 45 104-114
SAINT MARGARET'S CHAPEL: 42
SAINT MILDRED'S CHURCH: 49
SAINT THOMAS'S CHURCH: 48
SARRE: 42 119
SCHOOLS: 23 80 92-101 116 132
  GRENHAM HOUSE SCHOOL: 99
  QUEEN BERTHA'S SCHOOL: 100
  WOODFORD HOUSE SCHOOL: 99
SCREEN: (see Rood Screen)

SEATING: 11 44
  (inc. Pews)
SEPULCHRE: 8 44
SESSES: (see TAX)
SETTLEMENT CERTIFICATES: 14
SHEEP: 10
SHOPS: 10
SHUART CHURCH: 23 42
SMUGGLERS: 115-119
"SMUGGLERS" RESTAURANT: 131 147
SPIRE: 11 43 56
  (inc. Steeple)
STOCKS: (see Cage)
TAXES: 1 64 74 82 87
  (inc. Fees, Rents, Collections, Sesses)
TIN-MONEY: 4
TITHES: 14 22
TOWER: 42 45
UNION: (see Workhouse)
VAULTS: 45
VERMIN: 85
VESTRIES: 14 57 68
  (inc. Vestry Meetings.)
VICARS: 9 39 44
VICARAGE: 10 62
VILLAGE CENTRE: 132
VOW AND COVENANT: 11
WALLS (of Church): 42
WANTSUM: 21 39 42 123
WAR (Memorials, Books, Service, Soldiers): 17-18 73
WATERLOO TOWER: 31
WAX HOUSE: 11 59-62
  (see also Candles)
WAYWARDENS: 14 123
WEATHER VANE: 11
WILIIAM III: 53-54
WILLS: 59-60
WINDMILL: 128 155
WINDOWS (in Church): 11 42 45
  (inc Rossetti)
WOODCHURCH: 9 172-174
  (see also Acol)
WOODFORD HOUSE SCHOOL: 99
"WOOL" BURIALS: 7
WORKHOUSE: 14 73 74 77 87 127
  (inc. Union at Minster)
  (see also Almshouses and Poor)